Meg Prowting is a Children and Youth Development Officer for the Methodist Church in Britain. Before this, Meg worked for twelve years in a large secondary school in Warrington, where she was Head of Religious Education.

Penny Fuller is a Children and Youth Development Officer for the Methodist Church in Britain. Her previous role was with Methodist Children as the 9–13 years Project Worker. Penny also has 24 years' experience as a volunteer working in a local church setting with children.

Mike Seaton has worked for the Methodist Church for 20 years. In 2008 he was appointed as the Director of Children and Youth. Before that, he was the National Youth Secretary (MAYC), a Training Development Officer and a Project Manager at a Youth Centre in Darlington in the North East. Mike has also worked for a Local Authority and the YMCA.

C000165163

Barnabas for Children® is a registered word mark and the logo is a registered device mark of The Bible Reading Fellowship.

Text copyright © Meg Prowting, Penny Fuller and Mike Seaton 2012
Illustrations copyright © Simon Smith 2012
The authors assert the moral right
to be identified as the authors of this work

Published by
The Bible Reading Fellowship
15 The Chambers, Vineyard
Abingdon OX14 3FE
United Kingdom
Tel: +44 (0)1865 319700
Email: enquiries@brf.org.uk
Website: www.brf.org.uk
BRF is a Registered Charity

ISBN 978 1 84101 854 6

First published 2012
10 9 8 7 6 5 4 3 2 1 0
All rights reserved

Acknowledgments
Unless otherwise stated, scripture quotations are taken from the Contemporary English Version of the Bible published by HarperCollins Publishers, copyright © 1991, 1992, 1995 American Bible Society.

Scripture quotations taken from the Holy Bible, New International Version, copyright © 2011 by Biblica, are used by permission of Hodder & Stoughton Publishers, a member of the Hachette Livre Group UK. All rights reserved. 'NIV' is a registered trademark of Biblica.

Scriptures quoted from the Good News Bible pblished by The Bible Societies/HarperCollins Publishers Ltd, UK © American Bible Society 1966, 1971, 1976, 1992, used with permission.

Scripture quotations from *The Message*. Copyright © by Eugene H. Peterson 1993, 1994, 1995. Used by permission of NavPress Publishing Group.

The paper used in the production of this publication was supplied by mills that source their raw materials from sustainably managed forests. Soy-based inks were used in its printing and the laminate film is biodegradable.

A catalogue record for this book is available from the British Library

Printed in Singapore by Craft Print International Ltd

Participate!

Helping young people explore discipleship and vocation

**Meg Prowting,
Penny Fuller
& Mike Seaton**

Endorsements for Participate!

The passion of young people compels them to look for a purpose in their lives and something or someone beyond themselves. *Participate!* responds to this God-given desire with an excellent resource that will both form and empower young disciples to serve Christ in the world and church. Churches with a history of excellent young ministries are permeated with a sense of mission to young people. What this resource does, that most do not, is to encourage the whole church to be involved in the young people's journey to discern the will of God in their lives.
Revd Dr Steven Emery-Wright, Lecturer in Missions, Cliff College

Our Lord wants children and young people to be full participants in the life of the church and God's mission to the world. This creative resource, full of ideas, offers the whole church ways of helping children and young people grow, hear God's call and take action. Use it. Participate!
The Rt Revd Paul Butler, Bishop of Southwell and Nottingham

This ground-breaking resource believes that young people can be an active and contributing part of the church today, and challenges us all to enable them to take their rightful place and truly participate. It encourages young people to take themselves and their faith seriously enough to consider their vocation; it gives them the concrete experiences and prayerful resources to do so.
Dr Sam Richards, Director of Oxford Centre for Youth Ministry

Contents

Foreword 7

Introduction 8

Reflecting on children's ministry 11

Participate! Session plans

Session 1: Who am I? 16

Session 2: Valued for who I am 22

Session 3: Understanding community 28

Session 4: Church as a community of believers 34

Session 5: Hearing God's call 40

Session 6: Serving God and others 45

Session 7: Try it! 51

Appendix One

Step-by-step flow chart 56

Reflecting on children's ministry (photocopiable A5 booklet) 57

Commitment to Participate! sheets 59

Volunteer placement form 62

Placement guidelines 63

Participate! evaluation form for group leaders and young people 64

Placement evaluation form for role holders 65

Ideas for creative prayer 66

Learning styles 67

Appendix Two: Worksheets for the sessions

Session 1: People match 70

Session 1: My avatar 71

Session 1: God's character Bible quotes 72

Session 1: Made in the image of God 74

Session 2: Characteristics grid 75

Session 3: Cartoon guide to the community of Israel 76

Session 3: 'Love your neighbour' scenario cards 80

Session 4: The orchestra of Christ 81

Session 5: 'Match the story' cards 82

Session 5: Hearing God's call 83

Session 6: 'Would you or wouldn't you?' cards 85

Session 6: 'Gifts and skills' cards 86

Session 6: Which task? 87

Session 7: Questions 90

Foreword

That most people choose to become Christians when they're young is beyond serious dispute. To be sure, people respond to God's love and the invitation to follow Jesus Christ at many times in life, but the majority first choose to do so as young people. This is true the world over.

The crucial task is, then, as it has been down the ages, what to do next. How is that initial openness to Christian faith to be taken seriously and developed? What does it mean to follow Christ, belong to communities of those who also follow him, and share with them in being God's agents who transform the world into the likeness of God's kingdom? Like all other disciples, young people do not instinctively know how to become part of the Christian faith, with its believing and belonging, its practices, traditions and opportunities; they must be taught, and like all learning that is splendidly multifarious thing full of examples, experiences and explorations.

This is why a resource like *Participate!* is so crucially important—important for the whole church of God and not just young people as part of it. *Participate!* rightly takes for granted vital things: that 9- to 14-year-olds give and receive, to the benefit of all; that they experience a call to be active Christian disciples and live and grow in that call of God now, rather than merely preparing for some future service or mission; that the Holy Spirit bears witness with their spirit that they are children of God.

Here, then, is a healthy and accessible mix of quality input, shared wisdom, good practice, helpful hints and stimulating reflection from expert and experienced practitioners. The result is more than a 'how to' resource, but is a 'let's become' vehicle for transformative discipleship. Enjoy. Explore. Expect challenge and blessing.

Martyn Atkins
General Secretary of the Methodist Church in Britain

Introduction

What is Participate?

Participate! is a programme to enable young people (9–14s) to gain the understanding and skills they need to live as disciples of Jesus in the 21st century and to explore how they can use the gifts God has given them to participate in God's mission today. It is a programme in which the whole church can be involved.

Why explore vocation with 9–14s?

Children and young people are called by God to serve, just as adults are. Therefore, mission and ministry are both for and with children and young people, as well as adults. We need to help our young people to understand the nature of calling and the importance of serving, and to see them as part of the journey of being a disciple. Young people can serve God, the church and community in a variety of ways, appropriate to their age and abilities, and this service can start now. For some, vocation may be a calling for life; for others, it may be about how they will serve God at a particular time, with the knowledge that they may be called to something different in the future. Our discipleship journey involves listening to God and discerning the ways we can serve best, using the gifts and skills given to us. Nine- to 14-year-olds are on the discipleship journey and need ways to explore what this means for them now as well as in the future.

Practicalities

As part of the Participate! programme, the young people will undertake seven sessions. Participate! sessions can be fitted into already existing weekly meetings and clubs, or a new group could be established to work through the material. Participate! can be run with just one young person or several. There needs to be a group leader to facilitate the sessions, and this person could be a children's or youth worker or volunteer. It is essential, however, to have more than one adult present at all times.

The seven sessions could be done over seven or 14 weeks, depending on the time available. After the last session ('Try it!'), the young people will have the opportunity to choose a task that they are interested in trying as a voluntary placement. This role can be in the church or the local community and can take place just in one particular week, or it can be spread over a number of weeks. The young people will work alongside someone from the church who is already performing the task. If they wish, the young people can then try out further roles. While the young people are in the process of carrying out their chosen placements, they will be encouraged to reflect on the role undertaken and what it means to serve others and God in that way.

Preparation

Use the step-by-step flow chart on page 56 to help you prepare for your Participate! programme. The chart can also be downloaded from the website www.barnabasinchurches.org.uk/extra-resources/.

Getting the church on board

For the material to have the maximum effect, the whole church needs to feel a part of the Participate! programme. Discuss the programme with the church leadership team before you begin, and use the 'Reflecting on children's ministry' section on pages 11–14 to help you work through the theological background. Multiple copies of these pages can be downloaded from the website www.barnabasinchurches.org.uk/extra-resources/ for use in a house group situation. Alternatively, you can photocopy pages 57–58 (Appendix One) back-to-back to create an A5 booklet.

Commitment sheets

Photocopy the three commitment sheets on pages 59–61, or download them from the website www.barnabasinchurches.org.uk/extra-resources/

There is one sheet for the young person, one for the group leader(s) and one for members of the congregation. It may be useful to have a church service in which Participate! is explained to the congregation, ending with each person being given a commitment sheet to sign as their response. Alternatively, the sheets could be filled in as part of a house group session in which the reflective material on pages 11–14 (or the A5 photocopiable version in Appendix One) is used.

The range of 'Try it!' placements available for the young people to choose from relies on the willingness of members of the congregation to get involved. Each church member will need to be able to support a young person over the duration of the placement by allowing him or her to try out their role in the church or community. At the outset of the programme, members of the congregation who undertake roles will be encouraged to take part by filling in a volunteer placement form. The completed forms need to be returned to the group leader before the final session. The sheets will be used to enable the young people to choose the roles they would like to try. Photocopy the volunteer placement form on page 62. You will also find helpful placement guidelines on page 63. (Both pages can be downloaded from the website www. barnabasinchurches.org.uk/extra-resources/)

Most denominations in Britain and Ireland will have their own child protection policies, procedures and training. Before commencing Participate! please ensure that all participants are familiar with the policy, know who the contact person is for child protection issues and know what they should do if they have a concern relating to child protection. Permission and registration forms must be completed before starting the 'Try it!' session of the Participate! programme.

Continuous communication between the young people and the church congregation about Participate! will help everyone to feel involved. The programme may also offer an opportunity for churches to reflect on the topic of vocation and calling, in line with what the young people are doing.

The sessions

Each session is designed to take the young person on a journey of discovery about God, themselves and their role within the church and community.

The first session explores identity and individuality; the second session builds on the first, looking at the value that individuals have in the eyes of God, and the value we place on ourselves. The third session explores the purpose of community, allowing the young people to reflect on what communities they belong to and God's role for us within communities. The fourth session looks specifically at living as a community of believers within a church context, what roles people play within the church and how the young people feel about the community.

Session 5 explores the concept of vocation and looks at stories of people who have felt called by God. It encourages the young people to think about how and when God calls us. Session 6 builds on the idea that we are all called into a relationship with God and called to serve others. This session explores the meaning of service and gives examples from both the church and the community. Session 7 is designed to prepare the young people for their chosen 'Try it!' placement by giving them guidance and encouragement in the choices they wish to make. This session encourages the group to think about who they are and what gifts and talents they have, and to recognise the importance of service. The 'Try it!' placements, which follow Session 7, allow the young people to put this learning into practice by giving them the opportunity to try out a role or task in the church or community.

Structure of the sessions

Each session has four sections, as follows.

- Introductory activity (warm-up)
- God
- Others
- Me

The sessions will always start with an introductory activity, but the sections about God, Others and Me may be in a different order from session to session.

You are encouraged to complete one activity in each of the four sections. There is a choice of three suggested activities in each section, designed to suit groups differing in size, age, ability and learning styles. (There is more information about learning styles on page 67.) From the options given, choose the activities that suit your group best. You may choose to adapt some of the activities to suit your group's specific needs. You may also choose to do more than one activity in each section, if you have time available.

In some sections there is a 'Step further' option. which is designed to allow the young people to think on a deeper level about some of the issues covered. This is dependent on the time available and interests of the group.

Session 7 is structured differently in preparation for the placements.

Challenge for the week

At the end of each session is a challenge to help the group to put into practice what they have been learning and thinking about. How well they managed the challenge could be discussed at the following session if appropriate.

Prayer

Prayer is an important part of any discipleship journey. You are encouraged to pray together as a group during the session, whether at the beginning, the end or an appropriate point during the session. There are creative prayer suggestions on page 66, giving ideas for praying together as a group.

Timing

Each session is designed to be covered in a 90- to 120-minute time slot. However, if you have less time, you may choose to split each session into two 45-minute slots. This could mean that you complete the first six sessions in twelve weeks rather than six weeks. It is better to cover the material over a longer period of time than to miss out material from the sessions. (Do remember that you are not expected to cover all three activity suggestions in each section of the sessions.)

Planning

At the beginning of each session, there is a planning sheet designed to help you think through which activities you will choose, and how long you want to spend on them. There is also a space to list any equipment you may need and some questions to help you reflect on each session after you have completed it. The questions may provide a useful tool in planning further sessions.

The journal

The journal should be seen as an integral part of the journey of vocational exploration rather than as an add-on. It will help to build the skills of reflective practice as well as embedding faith exploration as part of home life alongside what takes place at church. Ideally, each participant will have their own copy of the journal. During the week following each session, it is hoped that the young people will work through the questions and activities in the journal. This will be done at home, where they will have time and space to reflect upon the issues discussed in the session.

Allow opportunity at the beginning of each session for the young people to feed back thoughts, questions or ideas coming from their journal, if they wish. The journal becomes the property of the young person, however. It is private and should be respected as such unless the young people choose to share their thoughts. It is worth reminding the group that if they have questions or issues that are raised by the activities in the journal, they may like to talk them through with someone they trust, such as the minister, a group facilitator, family member or other appropriate person.

Colour wheel

On the inside back cover of the journal, there is a colour wheel (see also the inside back cover of this book for reference). When young people are asked a question about how they feel, sometimes the answer is hard to put into words. The wheel helps us to describe feelings in terms of colours. The warm colours—red, orange and yellow—might make us feel warm or hot when we look at them. Warm colours might also make us feel active, energised or excited. The cool colours are green, blue and violet. These colours might make us feel cool, alone, sad or quiet.

Beginning the sessions

At the beginning of the programme, make sure the young people understand the structure and the aim of the sessions. Discuss the commitment sheet with them, in terms of the role of the young people and the role of the group facilitator. Explain the role and purpose of the journal and set some ground rules for working together as a group, such as respecting each other, listening to each other, and so on.

Evaluation

Photocopy the evaluation form on page 64 or download it from the website, www.barnabasinchurches.org.uk/extra-resources/. The form should be used by the church leadership team to assess the impact of the programme and decide what changes may need to take place to run the programme again. Also, it may give an opportunity for churches to evaluate the nature of involvement for children and young people in the life of the church. The church needs to think about further ways to support and encourage the young people who have worked through Participate! and have tried a volunteer placement.

Reflecting on children's ministry

For the programme to work well, the church as a whole needs to understand the theology that underpins the resource, and the responsibility—both collectively and individually—that church members have for the young people in the church. This chapter is designed to help you think theologically and practically about children's ministry and the contribution that the Participate! programme could offer. You could use this material as an individual, as part of a leadership team or in a house group session. The chapter is also available as a download from the website www.barnabasinchurches. org.uk/extra-resources. Read through the material and use the questions to stimulate reflection and discussion.

Bread and fish for all

After this, Jesus went across the Sea of Galilee (some call it Tiberias). A huge crowd followed him, attracted by the miracles they had seen him do among the sick. When he got to the other side, he climbed a hill and sat down, surrounded by his disciples. It was nearly time for the Feast of Passover, kept annually by the Jews.

When Jesus looked out and saw that a large crowd had arrived, he said to Philip, 'Where can we buy bread to feed these people?' He said this to stretch Philip's faith. He already knew what he was going to do.

Philip answered, 'Two hundred silver pieces wouldn't be enough to buy bread for each person to get a piece.'

One of the disciples—it was Andrew, brother to Simon Peter—said, 'There's a little boy here who has five barley loaves and two fish. But that's a drop in the bucket for a crowd like this.'

Jesus said, 'Make the people sit down.' There was a nice carpet of green grass in this place. They sat down, about five thousand of them. Then Jesus took the bread and, having given thanks, gave it to those who were seated. He did the same with the fish. All ate as much as they wanted.

When the people had eaten their fill, he said to his disciples, 'Gather the leftovers so nothing is wasted.' They went to work and filled twelve large baskets with leftovers from the five barley loaves.

The people realised that God was at work among them in what Jesus had just done.

JOHN 6:1–15 (*The Message*)

In the Bible, the story of the feeding of the five thousand appears in each of the four Gospels: Matthew, Mark, Luke and John. The accounts by Matthew, Mark and Luke are very similar to each other; John's account is the only one in which the five loaves of barley and two small fish are given to Jesus by a young boy.

Questions for reflection and discussion

- Why do you think only one Gospel mentions that the food was given by a child?
- Read the accounts in the other three Gospels (Matthew 14:13–21; Mark 6:30–44; Luke 9:12–17). What other aspects strike you from these accounts?

The New Testament reveals much about Jesus' life. The insight in John's account of the feeding of the five thousand helps us to appreciate Jesus' views about children and young people and, combined with an understanding of his teaching in this respect, provides the foundation on which ministry with children and young people should be based.

Bible texts that support our understanding of Jesus' attitude towards children include the following.

The Word became a human being and lived here with us (John 1:14).

Let the children come to me! Don't try to stop them. People who are like these little children belong to the kingdom of God (Mark 10:14).

'I promise you this. If you don't change and become like a child, you will never get into the kingdom of heaven' (Matthew 18:3).

'It will be terrible for people who cause even one of my little followers to sin. Those people would be better off thrown into the deepest part of the ocean with a heavy stone tied around their necks!' (Matthew 18:6).

Through these verses we recognise that:

- Jesus didn't enter the world as an adult but as a baby. He had first-hand experience of the life of a child at that time, and he knew the pressure and fears that they face.
- Jesus valued children and young people. He believed that, no matter what their age or ability, they had gifts that he could use for the benefit of others.
- Jesus believed it was the responsibility of the community of believers to enable children and young people to encounter God.
- Jesus knew that life for a child or young person is hard. He directed adults to keep young people safe and to nurture them on their spiritual journey.

Questions for reflection and discussion

- What are your thoughts about Jesus' attitude towards children?

For many churches, the Sunday school environment is the main focal point for teaching children and young people about the Christian faith. When Robert Raikes initiated the Sunday school movement in 1780, some people regarded Sunday schools as an early form of evangelism; some suggested that they were about the indoctrination of children, while others believed them to be about the mass education of the working classes, which (they thought) could ultimately threaten the hierarchy of Britain.

Sunday school lessons consisted of instruction on the Bible and the catechism—an uncomplicated book in the form of questions and answers, containing a summary of the principles of the Christian faith maintained by a particular church. Sunday schools were evangelistic in the sense that, through Christian education, children and young people were expected to experience an encounter with God and become part of the Christian faith.

Christians have different points of view about Christian education, its purpose, the theology (thoughts and beliefs about God) that underpin it, and how it should be delivered. These views shape the way we hear God's story and share it.

Questions for reflection and discussion

- What are your memories of your time in Sunday school or of the way your faith was taught through school?
- When and where did you learn the most about your faith? Was it when you were a child?
- When were you the most interested in the Christian faith?
- What do you think the purpose of Christian education should be?

Many people, like those who started the early Sunday schools, believe that we hear God's story only through the Bible and church traditions. Others, however, believe that personal experience and reason (what is reasonable or logical or makes sense based on our scientific understanding) influence the way God's story is heard and understood.

If we do not hold these theological influences—scripture, tradition, personal experience and reason—in balance, but focus too heavily on any single one, we end up not fully understanding God's story and not presenting it in a way that makes sense. We also restrict the way we live our Christian lives.

Some churches assume that, in order to pass Christian traditions and faith between generations in a consistent way, the methods used must remain the same. This ignores the fact that society has changed, that there are now many subcultures and that people learn in different ways.

Questions for reflection and discussion

- How has society changed since you were a child?

Christian ministry with children and young people must enable a connection with God, the world and each other, so that young people can think as disciples, talk as disciples and be disciples.

Nowadays, the accounts of many churches, Sunday school workers, children and young people suggest that this connection is achieved with varying degrees of success.

> ## Questions for reflection and discussion
>
> • Why do you think churches are successful or unsuccessful in their ministry with young people?

Although church attendance is declining, there is an anomaly in that many children and young people are baptised (or dedicated). At these services, members of each Christian community make promises to the child, to help him or her grow in faith and in the knowledge and love of God.

> ## Questions for reflection and discussion
>
> • Why do you think so many people who are unconnected with the church want their children to be baptised?
> • What can the church do to offer ongoing support to families who seek baptism for their children?

The Christian nurture of children and young people is the responsibility of the whole church. Jesus emphasises this in his teaching. Faith development in young people is extremely important; it requires an integrated approach and the emphasis should be on Christian nurture and growth.

Living as a disciple requires a commitment to worship, prayer, discipline and service. It involves reflecting on God through the influences of the Bible, tradition, experience and reason.

> ## Questions for reflection and discussion
>
> • Which of these four do you find the most useful in your own faith development, and why?

The Christian faith cannot be learnt. Churches need to direct their ministry so that young people can grow as disciples with a balanced approach to theology and within a Christian community that values, understands and affirms them. The American author and speaker Lawrence O. Richards suggests the following five processes for faith development.

1. Belonging to a faith community: Young people need to feel as if they are a part of an authentic faith community that models the messages they are given, helping them to give and receive love, which is essential to developing faith.

2. Participating in a faith community: Young people need to experience what it means to serve as well as to be served; this is how their faith will become living and life-influencing.

3. Modelling on people in the faith community: People in leadership roles have an influence over the lives of young people. If young people consider them to have honesty and integrity in the way they share their faith and live their lives, they will identify with them and emulate them.

4. Instruction in the word of God: The Bible needs to be an integral part of everyday living. It is important to understand its context, to explore the multiple messages it may convey and to be able to apply it to everyday living.

5. Opportunities for responsible choices: Young people need opportunities to practise their faith in a safe and supportive environment, and to question and challenge without fear of rejection or rebuke.

The Participate! programme is based on these five processes of faith development. It is a challenging approach, which requires a commitment from the church community, church workers and the young people themselves.

> ## Questions for reflection and discussion
>
> • Think about the five ways of developing faith. Do you recognise any of them in your own journey of faith?
> • Which of the five ways is currently seen in the children's and youth ministry at your church?

Participate! enables young people to explore vocation and calling, to discover how they can serve God and others today. Allowing opportunities for this to happen is an important part of children's and youth ministry.

> ## Questions for reflection and discussion
>
> • Who or what has helped (or helps) you to explore your calling?
> • How easy is it for you to exercise your vocation in your current situation?
> • How does the idea of being called by God make you feel?

Think about your church's ministry with children and young people.

- Who is it trying to reach?
- What is its purpose?
- How can your whole church become more involved in the children's and youth ministry that is taking place (or could take place)?
- How can you personally make a difference to the discipleship journey of the children and young people at your church and in your community?

> In the light of the above, if your church has a catechism or a statement of faith, do you know what it is and why the church feels it is necessary? Do you think it works for the 21st century? What questions and answers stand out for you? What might you change, and why?

Finally, read through the information about the Participate! programme. You may need to re-read or photocopy the three paragraphs headed 'What is Participate?', 'Why explore vocation with 9–14s?' and 'Practicalities' on page 8, which explain the basis for the programme. In what ways could you as an individual and as a whole church be involved in the programme? How could you make the programme sustainable so that it is not just a one-off experience?

Participate!

Session plans

Session 1

Who am I?

Planning sheet

Reminder...	
What preparations do you need to make for the room, refreshments, and so on?	

Prayer	
When and how will you pray during this session? (See ideas for creative prayer on page 66 for help.)	

Introduction to the programme

Discuss the structure of Participate! Hand out and explain what to do with the journal. Photocopy, hand out and discuss the commitment sheet.

Introductory activity

Activity option	Time allocated	Equipment and materials

Me

Activity option	Time allocated	Equipment and materials

God

Activity option	Time allocated	Equipment and materials

Others

Activity option	Time allocated	Equipment and materials

Total time allocated _____

Reflection on the session

- How did the group respond to the activities?

- What went well?

- Did the timings work?

- What needs to be reinforced in the next session?

- What was learnt that will be useful for planning in the future?

- If the session is to be run over two weeks, what material was covered and what still needs to be covered? (Make a note.)

- What else has the content of this session made you think about?

Who am I?

Programme

This session explores the issue of identity: who we are, the effect our identity has on ourselves and others, and what the Bible has to say about us as individuals.

Introductory activity

It is important that the group members are given the opportunity to be introduced to each other at the beginning of the first session. Below are suggestions for ways to do this. Choose one option that best suits your group, followed by the 'Step further' activity. By the end of the activity, the participants should know more about each other, as well as having had the opportunity to think about their own personalities.

Option One

On separate pieces of paper, each person in the group anonymously writes down one fact about themselves. (For example, 'I am grumpy in the mornings', 'I support Manchester United', and so on.) All the pieces of paper are collected, then they are read out in turn, and the group has to guess which member is being described by each fact.

Option Two

Divide the group into pairs. One person in each pair has a minute to find out as much information about their partner as they can by asking them questions that can only be answered with a 'Yes', 'No' or 'Can't say' response. (For example, 'Do you have brothers?') Swap partners and repeat the exercise a few times.

Option Three

Photocopy the 'People match' sheet on page 70 or download it from the website www.barnabasinchurches.org.uk/extra-resources/, and give a copy to everyone in the group. Encourage the young people to move among each other, trying to find people to match the statements on the sheet. The aim is to encourage conversation and confidence among the group. When a match has been found, the person's name can be written inside the square. The game can continue until the first person announces that all their squares are complete or that they have one complete line. Alternatively, you could have a time limit and see who has the most squares filled in by the end of the time allocation.

 Step further

The feedback after your chosen activity allows the young people to think about what they have heard from others and what they have said about themselves. The following questions may be useful discussion starters.

- On a scale of 1–10, how much do you think the group knows about you now?
- Do you think anyone ever will know everything about you? Who knows you best?
- What piece of information about other people in the group have you found the most interesting? Why?
- How much can be told about somebody just from what they look like or sound like?

Me

What we look like on the outside plays an important part in our self-identity and self-esteem. This section aims to find ways to explore what each person's character is like on the inside, rather than focusing on their outward appearance. Below are three suggestions. Choose one that is most appropriate for your group, followed by the 'Step further' activity.

Option One

Buy (or borrow) some mirrors. If possible, have enough for one each. Encourage everyone to look at their reflection in the mirror and then write on the mirror words that describe their personality. (Use an appropriate pen or crayon or a lipstick that can be wiped off afterwards.)

Option Two

If you have ever played on a games console, you will be familiar with making an avatar of yourself. Give everyone a copy of the 'My avatar' sheet on page 71 (which can also be downloaded from www.barnabasinchurches. org.uk/extra-resources/) and invite them to add words or images from the list, that describe their personality, to the space around the avatar.

Option Three

The TV character Doctor Who 'regenerates' from time to time—that is, the character takes on a new body but is still, in essence, the Doctor. Show a clip from one of the *Doctor Who* programmes in which he regenerates. Outline the point that, although he looks different on the outside, he is still 'the Doctor' on the inside. Ask the question: what makes him still 'the Doctor' if he looks different? Use the discussion questions in the 'Step further' section to explore this idea some more.

 Step further

- Can we still be who we are if our body looks different (for example, if we were injured or disfigured)?
- Which is more important to who we are—what we look like or what our character is like?
- When do we become who we really are? Is it at birth, or do we slowly develop into becoming our real selves?

God

This section focuses on two key Bible passages: Genesis 1:26 (being made in the image of God) and Psalm 139:1–16. Both of these passages help us to understand that we have a unique place in creation: God created our identity and we have a special relationship with him. You could explore both passages or just choose the one that best suits your group. Choose the activity option below that is most appropriate for your group.

Option One

For this exercise, try to make your meeting room a calm space. You may choose to have a candle to focus on, or some appropriate music playing in the background.

Read Psalm 139:1–16 out loud, slowly and carefully, and then repeat it. As you are doing so, encourage the group to close their eyes and listen carefully to the words. Ask them to think about any images or colours that come to their minds while they are listening. You may want to talk about this at the end of the reading. Ask them if there were any words or phrases that particularly caught their attention. Discuss with the group how this made them feel.

To follow up, you may wish to invite the group to draw a picture of their response to the psalm. Alternatively, they could make a PowerPoint slide show to set the words of the psalm to music, and use images they felt were appropriate to reflect their thoughts and feelings.

Option Two

Explain that Genesis 1:26 is part of the story of creation. Having created the world, vegetation and animals, God creates human beings as the pinnacle of his creation. In this context, explore the idea of our being made in God's image. Read Genesis 1:26 or have it displayed. Ask for the group's initial reactions or questions about the verse. One way to understand the meaning of our being made in God's image is that we don't physically look like God, but that we share a likeness with God. We resemble or reflect the qualities of God. Humans are the only species made in God's image and therefore we have a unique place in creation and a special responsibility.

To explore what it means for us to be made in God's image, we need first to explore what the qualities of God are. When there is a basic understanding of God's identity, the group can explore what it means to be made in his image. Ask them for suggestions as to what qualities they think God has. You could use the list below to help if they are struggling for ideas.

- Creative
- Wise
- Good
- Righteous
- Just
- Loving
- Forgiving
- All-powerful (omnipotent)
- All-knowing
- Holy
- Faithful
- Merciful
- Eternal

Either write the qualities up as a list or write each one on a separate piece of paper.

If you have a lively group, you may want to write the qualities on small pieces of card and hide them around the room. Then set the group to find them, the winner being the one who has found the most. Afterwards you could ask them how many of the qualities they showed while trying to find the pieces of card!

Photocopy the Bible quotes about God's character on pages 72–73, or download them from the website www.barnabasinchurches.org.uk/extra-resources/. Cut the quotes up to separate them and ask the group to match them to the qualities of God that they have identified. (The qualities can be matched with more than one Bible quote.) Again, if you have a lively group, you could turn this into a competition, working in teams to see who can match up the qualities with the Bible verses in the shortest time.

Photocopy the 'Made in the image of God' sheet on page 74, or download it from www.barnabasinchurches. org.uk/extra-resources/.

Invite the group to think about the questions either individually (in which case you will need one piece of paper per person) or in small groups. A large sheet of paper (flipchart size) could be used so that everyone can write their own ideas on the one sheet as a whole-group exercise.

Option Three

Write the following verses on sheets of paper.

- You created every part of me (Psalm 139:13, GNB).
- 'You did not choose me. I chose you' (John 15:16).
- God said, 'Now we will make humans, and they will be like us' (Genesis 1:26).
- 'I'll be with you. I won't give up on you; I won't leave you' (Joshua 1:5, The Message).
- 'I, the Lord, created you… I have called you by name; now you belong to me' (Isaiah 43:1).
- 'Before I shaped you in the womb, I knew all about you. Before you saw the light of day, I had holy plans for you' (Jeremiah 1:5, The Message).
- 'I have always loved you, so I continue to show you my constant love' (Jeremiah 31:3, GNB).

Read the verses together and talk through any questions the group may have. Have two pieces of paper for the group to write on. On one, write down what the verses teach us about God and, on the other, write what the verses teach us about ourselves. You could follow this up by asking members of the group to decide which of the verses they like the best and which make them feel the most special. If you had the verses written on separate pieces of paper, they could take their chosen verse home with them.

Others

This section explores how our identity impacts other people and how other people's identity impacts us. Choose the option below that is most appropriate for your group.

Option One

Ask the group questions to open up the idea that sometimes we may hide or change ourselves to fit in with others. The answers may be as follows.

- Yes
- Sometimes
- Perhaps
- Never

To make it more fun, label the four corners of the room with the above words. As you ask the questions, the young people stand in the corner that represents their answer. Below are some suggested questions, but you can add more.

- Do you wear clothes because they are fashionable?
- Would you ever consider plastic surgery to change parts of your face?
- Would you change your hairstyle if people had laughed at it?
- If you were being bullied at school, would you tell someone?
- Would you ever get a tattoo?
- Do people who have made a difference to the world inspire you to take action or make a difference too?
- If your friends smoked but you didn't like smoking and thought it was wrong, would you tell them how you felt?
- If you lived in a different country where you were treated badly for being a Christian, would you hide your faith?
- Would you tell people at school that you go to church?

If appropriate, while they are standing in the corners, ask the young people to explain or go into more detail about their answers.

Option Two

If possible, watch the clip from *Shrek* where Princess Fiona hides her real identity from Shrek, or watch a clip from *Spiderman* where he hides his true identity from other people. (If you cannot show a clip, you could simply talk about them, as most people are likely to be familiar with these films.) After watching, use the following questions to prompt a discussion.

- In the film *Shrek*, the character Donkey is not afraid to be himself; he doesn't hide who he is. Why do some people pretend to be something else?
- Do you think people always like themselves?
- What sort of things do you hide from your friends? Why do you think you do that?

Option Three

Read through the following story, and pause at the point where it says, 'What will Jason do next?' Ask the group how they think the story will end.

Jason is a very popular boy at school. He is on the football team, he mixes with the 'in crowd', many of the boys look up to him and many of the girls are after him! Alex is in the same class as Jason but, in many ways, is the complete opposite. Alex is regularly picked on for being a geek, and some of the class like to tease him because he goes to church. Alex has been unhappy for a while and often finds himself alone at lunch times. Recently, Jason has started going to his local church, having become interested in the Christian faith after discussions at his youth club. He has not told his friends yet because he is not sure how they will react. Jason soon realised that he goes to the same church as Alex and, although they don't know each other very well, they have started chatting together after church.

One lunch time, the boys in the class are making fun of Alex. They are calling him names like Bible Basher and shaking the contents of his bag on to the floor, saying that they're looking for his Bible and his cross. One of the boys shouts over to Jason to come and join them. Jason doesn't realise what is going on as he strolls over. When he sees what is happening, he knows he should do something but he just freezes!

What will Jason do next?

Jason bends down and starts picking up the contents of Alex's bag and carefully putting them back in.

'Everyone's entitled to have their own beliefs,' he says. 'You have yours, I have mine and Alex has his. You can't go around picking on people just because they have a different belief to you. Leave him alone!'

With that, Jason walks away from the group, who are now silent.

If you have a group that likes acting, invite everyone to act out what they think the ending of the story will be.

After the story has been told, discuss the following questions:

• How does this story make you feel?
• Should Alex have hidden the fact that he went to church?

• If you were Jason in the story, what would you have done and why?
• Do you admire Jason for what he did?
• Has anyone, or any situation, inspired you to behave or think differently?

Challenge for the week

Think about how you could influence people in a positive way this week by being yourself.

Valued for who I am

Planning sheet

Reminder...	
What preparations do you need to make for the room, refreshments, and so on?	

Prayer	
When and how will you pray during this session? (See ideas for creative prayer on page 66 for help.)	

Introductory activity		
Activity option	Time allocated	Equipment and materials

God		
Activity option	Time allocated	Equipment and materials

Others		
Activity option	Time allocated	Equipment and materials

Me		
Activity option	Time allocated	Equipment and materials

Total time allocated _____

Reflection on the session

- How did the group respond to the activities?

- What went well?

- Did the timings work?

- What needs to be reinforced in the next session?

- What was learnt that will be useful for planning in the future?

- If the session is to be run over two weeks, what material was covered and what still needs to be covered? (Make a note.)

- What else has the content of this session made you think about?

Session 2

Valued for who I am

Programme

This session explores the value we have to God, how we value others and the value we place on ourselves.

Recap

Ask the group what they can remember about the last session. What did they discover about God and themselves?

Journal

Invite the young people to share what they thought about when writing up their journal, Did anyone write a poem or a song that they would like to share?

NB: It is important to make it clear that this is entirely voluntary and that the journal is private unless people feel comfortable sharing parts of it.

Introductory activity

Choose the option below that is most appropriate for your group.

Option One

Invite the group to imagine it is the year 2095 and they are going to start a new life on the moon. They will be going with their family and they can take one small suitcase of belongings with them. What would they take? What is so valuable to them that they wouldn't want to leave it behind? Discuss why these items are important to them and why they would want the items with them for their new life on the moon. Take a small bag of your own, filled with your valuables, as a visual aid to start the discussion.

Option Two

Together as a group, make a list of things that are of value to the young people (remember to include items such as family, friends, good health, and so on, as well as money and possessions). Display the list on the wall so that everyone can see it.

Tell the young people that they have an imaginary £50 that they can spend at an auction to buy things of value on the list. The leader takes on the role of auctioneer. The bidding for each item starts at £10 and goes up by £10 a bid. The young people will need to decide which item(s) they want to bid for, as they will not be able to 'buy' everything. Therefore, they will be working out what is of most value to them. Once they have spent their £50, they cannot bid for anything else.

Afterwards, discuss whether what they bought was really of the most value to them. Encourage them to think about the items that they didn't get and what their life would be like without these things.

Option Three

For this activity, the young people are given a choice of two options. Label one end of the room as Option One and the other end of the room as Option Two. The young people stand at the end of the room that matches their choice. Below are some suggestions, but you can add more.

Which would you rather have?

1. A mobile phone	2. An iPod
1. Lots of money	2. Good health
1. A happy relationship	2. Being famous
1. Friends	2. Family
1. Friends	2. Good health
1. Education	2. A nice place to live
1. A one-week holiday abroad	2. A two-week holiday in the UK
1. Freedom of speech	2. Wealth
1. A job earning good money	2. A job that makes a difference to the world

God

This section explores the idea that God values us for who we are, regardless of the imperfections that we may think we have. Two main passages could be explored. Matthew 10:29–31 tells us that God knows every hair on our head, indicating the immense value we have to him. Luke 19:1–10 recounts the story of Zacchaeus, a man who was shunned by his own community yet proved to have value in Jesus' eyes. You could explore both passages or just one.

Option One

Set out a bowl of lemons, making sure there are enough for each person to have one. Each person takes a lemon from the bowl. Give everyone one minute to study their lemon in detail, in the hope that they will be able to recognise it again later. All the lemons are then put back in the bowl. Next, pass the bowl round again and invite everyone to try to pick out their own lemon.

It may be possible to do this, but if you had to recognise ten lemons or 100 lemons that were yours it would be much harder. Make the point that, if we take the time, we can get to know small details, but it is hard to know every detail about a lemon. It is harder still, if not impossible, to know everything about a person.

Read Matthew 10:29–31 slowly and carefully and then repeat it. Ask the question: If you had to choose three words to describe how you felt when you heard that verse, what would your words be?

Learning and reciting Bible verses is often seen as an old-fashioned approach, but it can still be of immense value and a powerful experience. It's a tradition that has been used for centuries and it is a way of carrying the Bible with you in your mind and heart wherever you go.

Make learning verses a fun and enjoyable experience. Set a challenge: in the space of three minutes, how much of Matthew 10:29–31 can the group remember accurately (preferably working in pairs). Make it a competition to see who can recite the most without making a mistake. While one person is reciting, invite everyone else to follow the passage to see if any mistakes have been made. If you have a competitive group, they will want to keep trying until they get it right.

Option Two

Many people think that they have to be perfect to be of value to God. The story of Zacchaeus shows that this is not the case. To understand why, we need to know the background to the story. Zacchaeus was a tax collector and his fellow citizens, the Jewish people, knew that he was a thief and a cheat. Zacchaeus worked for the occupying Roman forces and, because of this, he lacked all kind of respectability. No one expected Jesus to speak to someone like Zacchaeus. However, Jesus not only spoke to Zacchaeus but even asked to visit him in his home. This would have been quite scandalous at the time.

Explain the background to the group before reading the story in Luke 19:1–10. Encourage the young people to get into the story and imagine that they are watching it unfold. (This is why the background to the story is important.) Ask the group to think about how Zacchaeus might have been feeling at the time. You may choose to invite the group to act out a conversation between Zacchaeus and Jesus, using facial expression, tone of voice and body language to express how the characters might have been feeling. Also, you may like to discuss what other possible endings the story could have had. Then think what the consequences of those endings may have been.

Draw out the fact that God values all people, even those who are seen to be imperfect or worthless. There is a place for Zacchaeus with Jesus and, in their meeting, Zacchaeus undergoes a complete transformation.

Option Three

Our fingerprints are unique and can be seen as an important part of our identity. Our fingerprints can remind us of how special and unique we are to God. A number of activities could be done using fingerprints.

- Look up the following Bible verses. (You may already have used these verses in Session 1.)

  - You created every part of me (Psalm 139:13, GNB).
  - 'You did not choose me. I chose you' (John 15:16).
  - God said, 'Now we will make humans, and they will be like us' (Genesis 1:26).
  - 'I'll be with you. I won't give up on you; I won't leave you…' (Joshua 1:5, THE MESSAGE).
  - 'I, the Lord, created you… I have called you by name; now you belong to me' (Isaiah 43:1).
  - 'Before I shaped you in the womb, I knew all about you. Before you saw the light of day, I had holy plans for you' (Jeremiah 1:5, The Message).
  - 'I have always loved you, so I continue to show you my constant love' (Jeremiah 31:3, GNB).

Let everyone choose one verse that makes them feel the most special. Write it on to a small piece of card and put a fingerprint on the back of the card as a reminder that the person is special to God.

- Put everyone's fingerprints on to one piece of paper to remind them that they are all special to God and should all be valued by each other. This paper could be displayed in the room where you meet.

- Invite everyone to make a key-ring, badge or 'credit card' with their fingerprint on it. They can keep this item with them as they go about daily life, as a reminder that they are special and valued by God.

Others

This section will begin to explore how and why we treat others differently. Choose the option below that is most appropriate for your group. You may also like to try the 'Step further' activity.

Option One

Gather a random selection of pictures of people from newspapers and magazines (make sure the pictures are not of well-known celebrities). Ask your group to say what they think the person in the picture does, what they are like, and so on, just from looking at their picture. Next, discuss why they came to those conclusions and talk about how we often use someone's appearance to judge what they are like and the value they have.

Option Two

One of the most famous clips from the TV show *Britain's Got Talent* is of contestant Susan Boyle. When she came on stage to do her audition, the audience laughed at her. By the time she had finished singing her song, the audience were on their feet applauding. Watch the clip on YouTube: www.youtube.com/watch?v=RxPZh4AnWyk. The following questions may be useful in discussion:

- Why were people laughing at Susan Boyle?
- For what reasons are we most likely to judge a person? (For example, looks, background, wealth, accent, and so on.)
- Why do we judge people?
- How can we stop ourselves from treating people differently because they are not like us?

Option Three

Give out treats such as sweets, stickers, small toys, and so on, to some of the young people in your group, but deliberately miss others out. After a couple of minutes, when they have all finished eating or looking at what they have been given, ask those who weren't given a treat how they felt. Then ask those who did get the treat how they felt. In the discussion, draw out how it feels when some people are seen to be valued more than others.

 Step further

Use the following questions for discussion.

- Are there any groups of people in our community, school or church that are not treated with as much value as others?

- Why do you think they are seen as less valuable?
- What do you think God would say to people who are treated differently?

Me

This section challenges the young people to value themselves in the way that God values them. Choose the option below that is most appropriate for your group.

Option One

Photocopy the characteristics grid on page 75, or download it from the website www.barnabasinchurches.org.uk/extra-resources/. Cut out the boxes so that you have a set of small cards. Ask the group to sort the cards into two lists. The first list should contain what they consider to be good qualities in a person, and the second list should contain what they consider to be negative qualities in a person.

Afterwards, discuss the lists. Ask the group to think of any times when the negative qualities could actually be positive. Below are some of the characteristics that the young people may say are negatives, along with ways of showing that, in some situations, they can be positive characteristics. Try to encourage the young people to think of their own ideas first.

- **Outspoken**: sometimes people need to speak out against injustices and have their voice heard.
- **Lazy**: sometimes we need to be lazy and take time off to help us recuperate. God ordained that we should have a day of rest.
- **Rebellious**: sometimes we need to rebel against things that aren't right, such as unfair laws, prejudice and injustice.
- **Secretive**: sometimes Christians have to be secretive about their faith to protect themselves in countries where they would be persecuted. Even the first Christians met in secret.
- **Stubborn**: many people who have fought for the rights of others have had to campaign for many years, and being stubborn helps people to do this.
- **Lying**: sometimes people need to lie to protect others. For example, in World War II, a number of Christians helped Jewish people to escape from Nazi persecution. They would have needed to lie to save these people's lives.
- **Jealous**: sometimes feeling jealous shows how much you love someone. God is sometimes called a 'jealous God' because he demands our love (Exodus 20:5, NIV).

- **Angry**: sometimes people need to get angry about situations that are not fair or right. For example, the story of Jesus turning over the money changers' tables in the temple in Jerusalem shows that even he got angry (Mark 11:15–18).
- **Selfish**: sometimes we need to put ourselves and our own needs first, so that in the long term we may be able to do more to help other people. For example, someone may have been working very hard and reached the point of burn-out, so they decide to treat themselves to a relaxing holiday. This could be seen as selfish, as the cost of the holiday could have been used to help needy people, but the person will come back from their holiday refreshed and able to carry on helping others through the work they do.
- **Impolite**: Bob Geldof was famously impolite, but deliberately so, in order to shock people into donating money to help those in need.
- **Arrogant**: Moses was a humble shepherd who went to speak to the Egyptian Pharaoh to tell him to free the Hebrew slaves. It could be said that there was a certain arrogance in that!

You could ask your group to think about which of those characteristics they think they have. These answers will be quite personal, so you may like to reassure the group that they don't have to share them, but can just think about them privately.

Draw out the fact that what may be perceived as negative character traits could be seen as positive if used in the right way, and therefore we need a balance of traits. God has made us and can use our character traits for good. We need to value and make the best use of what God has given us.

Option Two

This exercise uses the questions below to draw out a creative response. Place a large piece of paper in the middle of the group and draw a line down the centre. Give each member of the group a pen. Ask the following question: 'Can you think of a time when you felt special or valued?'

Invite the group to draw their response to that question on one half of the paper (everyone draws on the same piece of paper). This is a personal response, so you don't need to discuss it first. You may want to give some ideas to help them get started, such as a drawing of a birthday cake, a Christmas tree, a football goal, a person singing on a stage, and so on. Each young person can contribute as many drawings as they like. After a couple of minutes, use the other half of the paper for the young people to draw their response to the next question: 'What did people say or do, or what happened to you, to make you feel valued?'

Suggestions for illustrating their response might be a drawing of a smile, a gift, people visiting, hands clapping in applause, and so on.

Repeat this process for the remaining four questions, using two more pieces of large paper, each divided into two.

- Can you think of a time when you have made someone else feel special or valued?
- What did you do to make that person feel special or valued?
- In what ways do we show that we value others?
- In what ways can we show that we value ourselves?

You may like to keep these pieces of paper displayed in the room where you meet.

Draw out the fact that we can show we value people in many different ways; it could be by giving someone a gift, or it could be by campaigning for the rights of someone in a different country whom we have never met. Also, recognising our own value is important: God values us and we should value ourselves.

Option Three

Use the following questions for discussion.

- We all have many characteristics that make up our identity. If each of us could choose one characteristic that we would like to have, or would like to use more positively, what would it be?
- If you used the story of Zacchaeus, ask what positive characteristics Jesus saw in Zacchaeus.
- Is it important that we value ourselves? Why?
- Is it hard or easy to believe that God values us? Why?

Challenge for the week

Think about how you could make other people feel special and valued this week.

Session 3

Understanding community

Planning sheet

Reminder...	
What preparations do you need to make for the room, refreshments, and so on?	

Prayer	
When and how will you pray during this session? (See ideas for creative prayer on page 66 for help.)	

Introductory activity		
Activity option	Time allocated	Equipment and materials

God		
Activity option	Time allocated	Equipment and materials

Others		
Activity option	Time allocated	Equipment and materials

Me		
Activity option	Time allocated	Equipment and materials

Total time allocated _____

Reflection on the session

- How did the group respond to the activities?

- What went well?

- Did the timings work?

- What needs to be reinforced in the next session?

- What was learnt that will be useful for planning in the future?

- If the session is to be run over two weeks, what material was covered and what still needs to be covered? (Make a note.)

- What else has the content of this session made you think about?

Session 3

Understanding community

Programme

This session is the first of two that will focus on community. The session will explore the nature of community. It will also allow opportunity to reflect on God's feelings about community, how communities are created, and the need to be transformed. It will encourage the young people to think about the communities they belong to and why.

Recap

Ask the group what they can remember about the last session. What did they discover about God and how we value ourselves and others?

Journal

Invite the young people to share what they thought about when writing up their journal. Is there anything anyone would like to share?

NB: It is important to make it clear that this is entirely voluntary and that the journal is private unless people feel comfortable sharing parts of it.

Introductory activity

Choose the option below that is most appropriate for your group.

Option One

A minimum of four people are required for this activity. Split the group into two teams and give each team a pen and paper. Read out a topic from the list below and give the teams 30 seconds to list as many things as possible that are associated with the topic. When the time is up, groups take turns to call out items from their list. They only get a point for items that other teams have missed.

- The pros and cons of social network sites: Facebook, Myspace, and so on.
- Different communities represented within the local neighbourhood.
- Jobs that people have in the community.
- What makes a good leader.
- The benefits of being part of a community.
- Things that all communities need.

Option Two

Mark a long line on the floor with masking tape. Mark a tick (to indicate 'agree') at one end and a cross (to indicate 'disagree') at the other.

Explain that you are going to read a number of statements, and the group members need to position themselves along the line at the point that best represents how they feel about a subject.

Invite people to explain why they are standing in that spot. When several people have spoken, give the group the chance to change position if they want to, and then ask why people might have moved.

Suggested subjects are as follows.

- Television soaps give a realistic portrayal of life.
- People should be careful about the information they post on social network sites.
- The age of voting should be lowered.
- All communities need leaders.
- Leaders need to demonstrate the best qualities.
- Communities need rules to exist.
- 'Community' is just another name for the neighbourhood you live in.

Option Three

Play a clip from *Toy Story* 1: start at 25:17 and stop at 28:30. Woody, a pull-string cowboy doll, is, in effect, the leader of a group of toys that belong to a boy named Andy. The toys come to life whenever humans are not around. Woody is Andy's favourite. When Andy is given Buzz Lightyear (a space ranger) for his birthday, Woody feels pushed out. Consumed with jealousy, he tries to get rid of Buzz.

Use the questions below to begin a discussion.

- Would you describe the toys as being a community? Why?
- Why do you think Woody behaved as he did? If you were Woody, how might you have reacted?
- Did the toys have an expected way to behave?
- What happened if one of the toys disobeyed the rules?

Here are the key points to draw out from options 1, 2 or 3:

- Community can be in a place such as a neighbour-hood.
- Community can be about a shared interest or a faith group.
- Community can be about families.
- People can be members of more than one community.
- Most communities have a leader.
- Communities need rules to exist.
- Communities have positives and negatives.
- Our understanding of community is influenced by the media.

God

God's desire for Israel was that they would be a people who would teach others about him. Israel was to be a faith community, a distinct nation that pointed others towards God and his promise to provide someone who would bring people back to God (the Messiah). For the most part, Israel failed in this task. God chose the nation of Israel to be the people through whom Jesus, the Messiah, would be born. After Adam and Eve disobeyed God (Genesis 3), God promised that the Messiah would come from the line of David, a descendant of Abraham (Matthew 1:1; see Genesis 12:1–3) to restore our relationship with God. God's ultimate purpose for Israel was fulfilled perfectly in Jesus. Choose the option below that is most appropriate for your group.

Option One

Give each person a copy of the cartoon guide to read. (This can be found on pages 76–79 or downloaded from www.barnabasinchurches.org.uk/extra-resources/.) You will need to elaborate on the story as you read through the cartoon. For an overview of the story, visit www.articlesbase.com/religion-articles/origins-of-Judaism-979494.htm. Ask the group to think of the key themes about God that they learn from the story in the cartoon guide. Possibilities might include the following.

- God gives his community a sense of identity and purpose.
- God provides leaders for his community.
- God sets the rules for his community to live by.
- God protects his community.
- God provides for his community.
- God did the impossible to create his community.

Copy each of the themes that the group identify (or from the list above) on to individual cards. The cards

can be used in one of the ways set out below. Select options that would work well with your group.

- Arrange the cards in order, starting with the activity that the group thinks is the most important for God to do, and finishing with the least important.
- Sort the cards to show the activities that the group thinks God still does today.
- Discuss the activities that the group thinks God should or shouldn't do.
- Which themes trigger the most questions? What are those questions? (For example, why did God create the community of Israel? Does God have favourites? How did God do the impossible, and why? Does God appoint leaders? What else do you think God should do for communities?)
- What are the positives and negatives of each theme? (For example, protecting a community may mean it will survive; appointing a leader may give direction but could mean that other people's ideas are ignored.)

Option Two

Give each young person a copy of the cartoon guide to read. (As in Option One, you will need to elaborate on the story.) Invite them to write the individual themes learned about God from this story on to separate sticky notes. Some possibilities are given below, but encourage them to add any others they may identify.

- God gives his community a sense of identity and purpose.
- God provides leaders for his community.
- God sets the rules for his community to live by.
- God protects his community.
- God provides for his community.
- God did the impossible to create his community.

Next, invite each person to stick his or her sticky note(s) on the section of the cartoon that best represents that theme. Ask the group to compare their cartoon guides and talk about the similarities and differences in their answers.

Option Three

God wants us to live in communities, but what should those communities be like? God wants us to love our neighbour—a basic principle for any community—but what does it really mean to love our neighbour in our community? Read Leviticus 19:18: 'Love your neighbour as yourself.' Photocopy the scenario cards on page 80, or download them from www.barnabasinchurches.org.uk/extra-resources/. Cut up the cards to separate them.
Place the cards face down on a table. Invite everyone

to take turns to choose a card and read it out to the rest of the group. Discuss what you could do to be a good neighbour, thinking of as many possibilities as you can, as there are a number of ways to be a good neighbour. Draw out the idea that sometimes we may act alone and sometimes we may need to join with a group of people to make a difference, and that sometimes being a good neighbour involves action and sometimes it is just about listening to people.

After you have talked about the scenarios, discuss which ones the group would find easy to do and which ones would be difficult. You could put the cards into two piles. Invite the group to think about the effect that being a good neighbour would have on them. (For example, it may take up their time; other people may dislike them; they might prefer to be doing something else, and so on.) Ask the young people to think about what the world would be like if everyone loved their neighbour.

Others

Living in a particular place makes us part of a community. This section may help you to think about what is happening in your community, where God might be at work in your community and what our roles and responsibilities are within and towards the community. Choose the option below that is most appropriate for your group.

Option One

Choose one of the following:

- Distribute copies of local newspapers to the group. These could be free papers or your local evening newspaper.
- Record a news bulletin from the local radio and play it to the group.
- Record the local television news or *Newsround* and watch it with the group.
- Visit the BBC news website for your region.

Based on the information you have chosen, ask the group to identify the issues affecting their community. Which people are affected by those situations, and how? How is God involved in those situations?

 Step further

Create a montage of pictures (hard copy or electronic) and use them as a basis for prayer about the issues you have identified, asking God to be at work in each and every situation.

Option Two

Share the following with the group.

'Join me' is the name given to a movement started in London by British writer Danny Wallace in 2002. Members of the movement are called Joinees. Danny was inspired by a relative who had once unsuccessfully attempted to build a peaceful community on his farm in Switzerland. Danny put an advert in a London paper asking readers to 'Join me'. All they had to do was to send one passport-sized photograph. The advertisement contained no other details and no reason for sending the photo. Danny said he had no plans about what he would do when people sent their photos. In fact, his only hope was that he could improve upon the number of people who had joined his relative—three!

According to Danny, 'It was a silly half-baked project. But thanks to a huge and diverse group of perfect strangers, it became something much bigger.' To Danny's surprise, the advertisement attracted a large number of people. As the group grew in number, Danny was put under pressure by its members to explain its purpose. Having had no reason in mind when he first asked people to join, Danny sought a purpose for his 'Joinees'. Ultimately, he presented the idea of performing random acts of kindness, preferably to a stranger, every Friday. Over time it has become accepted that the day of the week is not important, and that random acts of kindness may be performed whenever the opportunity presents itself.

Danny's 'collective' or community now has over 12,000 members and there have been books and websites produced about it.

Imagine that you were to start your own community.

- What would it do, that would have a positive impact on others?
- Would your community have a leader? If so, who?
- What rules or guidelines would you have?
- How would you get people to join?
- Would it have an open or closed membership?
- How would God be involved in this community?

 **Step further**

Read the story of the Ten Commandments (Exodus 20:1–17). Think about why God gave the people of

Israel these commandments. Why so many? Why did he not allow the people to think of their own?

Option Three

You may want to start this activity by watching an excerpt from one of the many television soaps, such as *EastEnders, Coronation Street, Home and Away, Neighbours, Hollyoaks* or similar. Each of these programmes tells the story of a particular community.

Read out the following scenario.

A local council has just created 45 houses on a new street called 'Windsor Street'. People have been selected from all sorts of backgrounds to live on the street. Some are families, some are single, most are employed but a few are retired or unemployed. Some have physical disabilities, some don't speak English as their first language, some are Christian, some have other religious beliefs and some have none. It is all part of a scheme to create new communities.

You are a member of a team of consultants called 'Community shapers'. You have been invited in by the council to give advice on how to get Windsor Street to become a community. What ideas do you have? (This can be done as a group or individual activity.)

Think about the role of the local church in this community. What does it do?

Me

Choose the option below that is most appropriate for your group.

Option One

Ask each person to make a list of the communities they are a part of. Invite everyone in the group to pair up with someone else and create a Venn diagram similar to the example below. (Venn diagrams are used to show what

things have in common, and what the differences are.)

Encourage everyone to choose one community and tell the rest of the group why they are part of it. Discuss whether there is a difference between a Christian community and a non-faith community.

Option Two

Make a pack of cards using the phrases below (one phrase per card). The group take turns to roll a dice. People throwing a 1 or a 6 must choose a card and complete the phrase. Invite people to add their own suggestions.

*   People belong to communities because…
*   Being part of a community makes me feel…
*   Being left out of a community makes me feel…
*   Christian communities are important because…
*   You know you are part of a community when…

Option Three

Invite everyone to draw a picture of a community they are a part of. Ask them to think about how that community could be improved.

 Step further

*   What is needed for a group of people to be a community?
*   Can a social network group such as Facebook or Bebo be a community?
*   Are any of the groups you belong to closed, secret or private? Is that acceptable? Should all communities be open?
*   What part might a young person's Christian faith play in each of the communities they are a part of?

Challenge for the week

Think of an idea for improving one of the communities you belong to, and then give it a try.

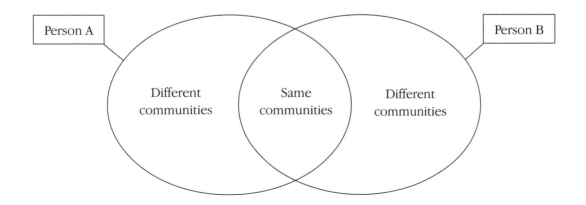

Church as a community of believers

Planning sheet

Reminder...	
What preparations do you need to make for the room, refreshments, and so on?	

Prayer	
When and how will you pray during this session? (See ideas for creative prayer on page 66 for help.)	

Introductory activity		
Activity option	Time allocated	Equipment and materials

God		
Activity option	Time allocated	Equipment and materials

Others		
Activity option	Time allocated	Equipment and materials

Me		
Activity option	Time allocated	Equipment and materials

Total time allocated _____

34

Reflection on the session

- How did the group respond to the activities?

- What went well?

- Did the timings work?

- What needs to be reinforced in the next session?

- What was learnt that will be useful for planning in the future?

- If the session is to be run over two weeks, what material was covered and what still needs to be covered? (Make a note.)

- What else has the content of this session made you think about?

Session 4

Church as a community of believers

Programme

This session explores the spiritual aspect of communities, the local church as a community, its role in witnessing and transforming the wider communities, and the duties and responsibilities we each have to the communities we belong to.

Recap

Ask the group what they can remember about the last session. What did they discover about God and themselves?

Journal

Invite the young people to share what they thought about when writing up their journal.

NB: It is important to make it clear that this is entirely voluntary and that the journal is private unless people feel comfortable sharing parts of it.

Introductory activity

Choose the option below that is most appropriate for your group.

Option One

The game 'funny bones' involves holding a bone of one person's body next to the bone of another person's body. For example, one person has to put their ankle bone next to the knee bone of someone else. Eventually, the whole group are connected, often with hilarious results.

Write out appropriate bones in the body on to A5-sized pieces of card. You will need to have twice the number of cards as you have players, but you can repeat what is written on the cards. Suitable suggestions would be: ankle bone, knee bone, toe bone, hip bone, shoulder bone, head bone, elbow bone, wrist bone.

- Line the group up.
- Player 1 picks a card at random; player 3 then chooses a card. The players have to connect at the bones

written on their cards. For example, two people may have to stand with player 1's elbow connected to player 2's ankle. To make sure the connection is kept, the cards have to be held between the two bones.
- Player 2 is then handed another card, and player 3 chooses a card. They then have to connect at the bones written on their cards, while keeping the connection with player 1.
- The process continues until all players are connected. You may choose to connect your last player back to the first.
- See how long they can last without dropping their cards!

Option Two

You will need photographs or pictures of different churches, paper, pens and pencils.

Show the young people the photographs of the churches. Give them one minute to look at the photos and then cover them up. Invite the group to draw what they can remember. Next, ask everyone to share their drawings with the whole group. What aspects did they focus on and why? Draw out the fact that people often regard the church as being a building. Although the buildings are of importance, the church is actually the Christian believers who gather there.

Option Three

Play one of the following DVD clips.

- *The Vicar of Dibley* (episode 1): when the old vicar of Dibley dies suddenly during Evensong, the bishop is quick to appoint a successor. The villagers are astonished to find that the new incumbent is a woman.
- Find a suitable clip from episode 2 of the first series of *Rev*. (*Rev* is a contemporary sitcom about the Reverend Adam Smallbone, a Church of England vicar, newly promoted from a sleepy rural parish to East London.) Episode 2 sees Darren, a charismatic evangelist, coming to Adam's church, bringing his congregation with him. Darren begins to make many changes to Adam's church.
- *Mr Bean* (series 1, episode 1, story 3): Mr Bean goes to church and tries to stifle a sneeze.

Ask the young people if they agree with the way the church is portrayed in the programme. Do they think it is accurate and fair? If so, why? If not, why not?

God

When God created the community of Israel, his plan was that they would show other nations how to live so that everyone could have a relationship with God. The community of Israel didn't fulfil all that God had hoped they might, so God needed another way to tell people of the value of being in relationship with him. Through Jesus, God again chose community—communities of believers (the Church).

This section will draw out the fact that the church is a community of Christian believers. Each person has a role to play and everyone supports the other members of the community: no one is more important than another, but, unless everyone works together and plays their part, the work of the Church will not be done. Choose the option below that is most appropriate for your group.

Option One

Give everyone a copy of the poem 'The orchestra of Christ', which is a paraphrase of 1 Corinthians 12:12–26. (Photocopy the text on page 81 or download it from www.barnabasinchurches.org.uk/extra-resources/.) Read it together in your group. Then encourage the young people to create musical instruments from everyday junk that you have assembled beforehand, such as margarine tubs, elastic bands, cardboard tubes, old saucepans, tin foil, pens that click—anything that would make different-sounding noises. This is best done by working in smaller groups, encouraging the need to share and cooperate.

When the instruments are complete, invite the young people to re-read 'The orchestra of Christ' and to play their musical instruments at appropriate times during the reading.

Alternatively, invite the group to provide a musical background to the reading by using body percussion. Traditionally, the four main body percussion sounds (in order from lowest pitch to highest pitch) are:

1. Stomp: stamping the feet against the floor or a resonant surface.
2. Patsch: patting the left, right or both thighs with hands.
3. Clapping hands together.
4. Click or snapping: clicking with the thumb and middle fingers.

There are also numerous other possibilities, including hitting the chest, whistling, slapping or flicking the cheeks with the mouth open, or clicking with the tongue against the roof of the mouth.

Use the following questions for discussion.

- Why did everyone make different instruments or sounds? Would it have mattered if everyone had chosen the same instrument or sound?
- What does it mean to play in harmony?
- Did everybody play at the same volume?
- How could your local church be like an orchestra?

Option Two

Rap music has often been used as a form of storytelling. Together, read 1 Corinthians 12:12–31 from *The Message* (below) and then invite the group to retell the passage by creating their own rap music.

You can easily enough see how this kind of thing works by looking no further than your own body. Your body has many parts—limbs, organs, cells—but no matter how many parts you can name, you're still one body. It's exactly the same with Christ...

A body isn't just a single part blown up into something huge. It's all the different-but-similar parts arranged and functioning together. If Foot said, 'I'm not elegant like Hand, embellished with rings; I guess I don't belong to this body,' would that make it so? If Ear said, 'I'm not beautiful like Eye, limpid and expressive; I don't deserve a place on the head,' would you want to remove it from the body? If the body was all eye, how could it hear? If all ear, how could it smell? As it is, we see that God has carefully placed each part of the body right where he wanted it.

But I also want you to think about how this keeps your significance from getting blown up into self-importance. For no matter how significant you are, it is only because of what you are a part of. An enormous eye or a gigantic hand wouldn't be a body, but a monster. What we have is one body with many parts, each its proper size and in its proper place. No part is important on its own. Can you imagine Eye telling Hand, 'Get lost; I don't need you'? Or, Head telling Foot, 'You're fired; your job has been phased out'? As a matter of fact, in practice it works the other way—the 'lower' the part, the more basic, and therefore necessary. You can live without an eye, for instance, but not without a stomach. When it's a part of your own body you are concerned with, it makes no difference whether the part is visible or clothed, higher or lower. You give it dignity and honour just as it is, without comparisons. If anything, you have more concern for the lower parts than the higher. If you had to choose, wouldn't you prefer good digestion to full-bodied hair?

The way God designed our bodies is a model for understanding our lives together as a church: every part dependent on every other part, the parts we mention and the parts we don't, the parts we see and the parts we don't. If one part hurts, every other part is involved in the hurt, and in the healing. If one part flourishes, every other part enters into the exuberance.

You are Christ's body—that's who you are! You must never forget this. Only as you accept your part of that body does your 'part' mean anything…

But it's obvious by now, isn't it, that Christ's church is a complete Body and not a gigantic, unidimensional Part? It's not all Apostle, not all Prophet, not all Miracle Worker, not all Healer, not all Prayer in Tongues, not all Interpreter of Tongues. And yet some of you keep competing for so-called 'important' parts.

1 CORINTHIANS 12:12–31 (*THE MESSAGE*)

Discuss together what we might learn about church from this passage.

Option Three

You will need newspaper, sticky tape, plain paper and pens.

Arrange the group into small teams. Each team is to build a bridge. Before starting the task, each person is to be given one of the roles listed below. (Explain that they must not share this role with any of the others in their team and they must carry out only this role.)

- Designer: You are to design a bridge that can stand alone, without support, made out of tubes of newspaper.
- Sticky tape monitor: You are in charge of the sticky tape and must keep hold of it at all times. You can only provide tape in lengths of 5cm, and only to the bridge builder and newspaper monitor.
- Newspaper monitor: You are in charge of rolling the sheets of newspaper into long tubes. You may use a small piece of sticky tape to stop them unravelling.
- Bridge builder: You are to build a bridge according to the design provided by the designer. You are not allowed to adapt it. You can only use the tubes of newspaper provided by the newspaper monitor, and you must get your sticky tape from the sticky tape monitor.

After the activity, ask the following questions.

- Did you like the role you were assigned?
- How important did you feel your role was? Very or not very important? Why?
- If you could have chosen a role, which one would it have been?

Read the following passage together.

Christ holds [the body] together and makes all of its parts work perfectly, as it grows and becomes strong because of love.
EPHESIANS 4:16

The local church is often described as the bridge between God and community. Each Christian believer has a role to play in helping the church to be that bridge into the local community; all of us are important.

Others

Introduce the concept that community is at the heart of the church. In the New Testament, the Greek word *ekklesia* has usually been translated in two ways—first by the term 'assembly', and second by the word 'church'. Jesus said, 'Whenever two or three of you come together in my name, I am there with you' (Matthew 18:20), and this means little assemblies of Christian believers meeting together and witnessing within the community. Choose the option below that is most appropriate for your group.

Option One

Have available a map of your local town. Ask the young people to mark on the map all the places where Christians meet together. These places will include traditional churches, but may also include house churches, community churches, Christian Unions and so on.

Use the following questions for discussion.

- Why do you think there are so many different places where Christians can meet together?
- What is the purpose of the church? (Worship, prayer, evangelism, service, and so on.)
- What are the advantages and disadvantages of large and small gatherings of Christians? (You could split the group into two and ask one group to focus only on big congregations, while the other group focuses on small congregations.)
- Do you think there should just be one big church rather than lots of smaller ones? If so, why? If not, why not?
- Does your church play an important role in your local community? If so, what is it?

Option Two

Paul was one of the early leaders of the church after the time of Jesus. He wrote a letter to the church members in Corinth to give them encouragement and advice on how to be a good church community. Invite the young people to write letters to their church to give encouragement and advice. (Ask the group if they would like to share the letters with the church. If so, think of an appropriate way to do this.)

Option Three

In many Communist countries, such as China and North Korea, Christians have not been allowed to meet together as 'church'. Often the church leaders are imprisoned and Bibles are taken away. Imagine that the British government has decided to make Christianity illegal from midnight tonight. Ask the group how they would feel about this. Would they be angry, sad, or not bothered? Why? Do they think they would still want to meet as a group? Why do people in countries where Christianity is illegal continue to meet when the risk could be death? How could we share the Bible with others, especially if we didn't have many copies? Is it important to share the Bible?

Me

Choose the option below that is most appropriate for your group.

Option One

Copy each of the following sentences on to separate pieces of A4 paper. Write the sentence at the top of the page.

- I think meeting with other Christians is important because…
- I think people need to help in church because…
- The worst thing about church is…
- The best thing about church is…
- Our church is important to our community because…
- The word that describes how I feel about church is…

Invite everyone to select a sentence randomly and write their response underneath the sentence on the paper. Gather the papers back in and redistribute them so that the young people respond to a different sentence. Repeat this process until everyone has written a response to each sentence. Invite the group to read and respond to the different answers that have been given.

Option Two

Cars that are over three years old are checked every year by mechanics to ensure they are roadworthy and safe. (This is called an MOT.) Imagine that you were doing a similar process for your church to check that your church is a healthy community. Discuss the following questions.

- Do you think that your church works well as a community of Christian believers? If so, why? If not, what needs to change?
- Does your church welcome new members? Do you yourself welcome new people?
- Do you feel a part of the communities within your church?
- Does your church set a good example to people who live nearby but do not go to your church? Do you set a good example to others?
- Your local church is a part of the worldwide Church. Does your church connect with other churches in the world—the global Christian community?
- Would you let your church pass its MOT?
- What can each one of us do to help the church become an even healthier community?

Option Three

Give each person two sheets of paper. On the first write, 'What I can give to my Christian community'. On the second write, 'What I'd like to receive from my Christian community'. Invite everyone to write their ideas on each sheet of paper. Then discuss the responses and circle the three that the group considers to be the most important.

Challenge for the week

Complete the Communities Questionnaire on page 27 of your journal. You'll need to have this with you for Session 6.

Hearing God's call

Planning sheet

Reminder...	
What preparations do you need to make for the room, refreshments, and so on?	

Prayer	
When and how will you pray during this session? (See ideas for creative prayer on page 66 for help.)	

Introductory activity		
Activity option	Time allocated	Equipment and materials

God		
Activity option	Time allocated	Equipment and materials

Others		
Activity option	Time allocated	Equipment and materials

Me		
Activity option	Time allocated	Equipment and materials

Total time allocated _____

Reflection on the session

- How did the group respond to the activities?

- What went well?

- Did the timings work?

- What needs to be reinforced in the next session?

- What was learnt that will be useful for planning in the future?

- If the session is to be run over two weeks, what material was covered and what still needs to be covered? (Make a note.)

- What else has the content of this session made you think about?

Session 5

Hearing God's call

Programme

This session looks at what happens when God asks people to do something specific. Some people refer to this as being 'called' by God. We sometimes hear Christians talking about their 'calling'.

Recap

Ask the group what they can remember about the last session. What did they discover about communities?

Journal

Invite the young people to share what they thought about when writing up their journal. Did anyone write anything they would like to share?

NB: It is important to make it clear that this is entirely voluntary and that the journal is private unless people feel comfortable sharing parts of it.

Introductory activity

Choose the option below that is most appropriate for your group.

Option One

Beforehand, prepare two empty and cleaned baked bean tins (or yoghurt pots) by drilling a small hole through the centre of the base of each one. Fasten the two tins together by passing a long piece of string through the holes and knotting it in place to secure it.

Each tin is held by a young person, with the string taut—if possible, with two tins in different rooms. One person speaks a message into their tin and the other person tries to hear what is being said by holding their tin to the ear. Try various messages with the string at different lengths. Although this may cause amusement, it raises the point that often it is hard to hear a message clearly and correctly.

Option Two

This activity will work well if you have a group that likes to be noisy. One person (player A) stands facing another person (player B), four to five metres apart. The rest of the group form a wall between the two players. Player A has to shout a message to player B. However, the people in the wall have to make as much noise as possible so that player B can't hear the message. Allow player A one minute to get their message across and then ask player B what they thought the message was. You can swap the players around and play this a few times.

Option Three

Offer two scenarios to the group and ask which one they would be more likely to say 'yes' to.

- You have been asked to represent your school at a major national event, celebrating the work in schools. Only three people have been chosen from your school to attend, and it will involve meeting a number of celebrities from TV, music and sport. Would you do it?
- You have been asked to spend Saturday helping to clean the house, starting with the bathroom, then your bedroom and finally the kitchen. Would you do it?

Use the following questions for discussion.

- Which option was easier to say 'yes' to, and why? Was it an easy decision?
- Does it make a difference who asks you to do something?
- Who would you find it difficult to refuse if they asked you to do something?

God

There are many stories in the Bible in which we see God calling people. He does it in a variety of ways and gets a variety of responses. God spoke to Moses through a burning bush, but Moses was anxious about what he was asked to do. Jonah refused to acknowledge God's call and actively avoided it. We read in the New Testament that Jesus called people to do certain tasks by speaking to them in person. The activities below are based upon the following three stories. You may like to familiarise yourself with the stories.

- Moses: Exodus 3:1–12
- Jonah: Jonah 1:1—3:3
- Peter walks on water: Matthew 14:22–31

Choose the option below that is most appropriate for your group. You may also like to try the 'Step further' activity.

Option One

Give out paper and a variety of coloured pencils to each member of the group. Read one of the above stories aloud. While you are reading, invite everyone to make an 'emotions graph' to chart the feelings of the main character in the story. (You may need to read the story twice.)

Label the vertical axis of the graph with the word 'happy' at the top and the word 'worried' or 'anxious' at the bottom. The horizontal axis shows the duration of the story. As you read the story, ask the young people to draw a line on their graph to show how the character may be feeling at particular points in the story. They can also use their coloured pencils to match parts of the story and associated feelings with particular colours. The use of colour is very subjective but an interesting way for the group to express their responses to the story.

Option Two

Watch a clip of one of the Bible stories on DVD. For example, *The Prince of Egypt* tells the story of Moses (watch the clip with the burning bush), and the 'Bible in Animation' series has episodes on Jonah and Moses. You may like to 'freeze-frame' the DVD from time to time in order to ask the group what they think the main character may be feeling at particular points, or how they would feel if they were that character.

If you don't have access to a DVD player, try acting out one of the stories. You could still get the group to 'freeze-frame' at certain points for a brief discussion.

Option Three

Photocopy the 'Match the story' cards on page 82, or download them from www.barnabasinchurches.org.uk/extra-resources/. Cut up the cards, mix them up, and ask the group to work out which cards match which story (Moses, Jonah and Peter). At the end, make sure everyone has the correct answers (the master sheet has the correct order in three labelled columns), as this will help the young people to begin to know the stories.

 **Step further**

Explore the stories in more depth, using the following questions for discussion.

- How does the story make you feel?
- If you had been the main character in the story, how do you think you would have felt?
- What questions would you like to ask the main character in the story?
- Why do you think God asks people to do things that they don't understand or don't want to do, or things that are difficult?
- Why does God call individuals when he could do the job himself?

Others

Photocopy the stories about people hearing God's call on pages 83–84, or download them from the website www.barnabasinchurches.org.uk/extra-resources/. The stories show some of the different ways in which God calls people. Below are three possible ways of exploring the stories and the young people's responses to them. Choose the option below that is the most appropriate for your group. You may also like to try the 'Step further' activity.

Option One

Give each person a piece of paper and a pen. Read out two or more of the stories from the sheet, but pause between each story. Invite the young people to note down one word that describes how they feel about the story while you are reading—for example, inspired, unconvinced, curious, disinterested, trusting, and so on.

At the end of each story, invite the group members to choose one of the words that they have noted down. Ask them to write it in large letters on their pieces of paper. Count to three, and then ask everyone to hold their piece of paper up and show their word to everyone else. Draw out why they have chosen that word to describe their feelings about the stories.

Option Two

Read the stories from pages 83–84 to your group. Write the names of the people in the stories on to pieces of card or paper. Set up a washing line using string, and peg the names of the people on to the line. Next, invite the young people to re-peg the names according to the instructions below. (This may require some discussion among the group.)

- Arrange the stories in historical order.
- Group together those people who you think had a similar experience of being called by God.
- Arrange the people in order, according to the stories you find the most inspiring.
- Arrange the people in order, according to the stories you find the most exciting.
- Arrange the people in order, according to the stories you find the hardest to believe.

Option Three

Imagine you could interview one of the people from the stories. Make a list of the questions you would like to ask them.

 Step further

Think about or discuss the following questions.

- Is your conscience the same thing as the voice of God?
- Does God call only Christians to do his work?

 Me

This section is designed to allow the group the opportunity to reflect upon God's calling for their lives. Explain that there are many ways to experience God's call. It could come through visions or dreams, hearing a voice, sensing, through the Bible, or through what other people say to us. Christians believe that everyone is called to be in relationship with God, and it is through our relationship with him that we realise our whole life is a calling to follow God's ways in ordinary, everyday events. However, sometimes God may have a very specific task for us. Choose the option below that is most appropriate for your group. You may like to follow up your choice with the 'Step further' discussion.

Option One

Use the clip from the film *Bruce Almighty* where Bruce gets called on his pager by God, or use the clip from *Evan Almighty* where Evan is asked to build an ark. Discuss how the characters responded to the call. How would the young people feel if they were Bruce? What prevents us from hearing God's voice?

Option Two

Watch the animation *Connect with the God*, available on vimeo at http://vimeo.com/14270590. The animation lasts approximately three minutes.

Option Three

It can be difficult for people to work out whether they are actually hearing God's call. The following activity illustrates how difficult it is to discern 'the real thing'. For this exercise, use different types of cola. The young people have to taste the cola and work out which one is the well-known brand. Alternatively, you could use a biscuit that has a brand name and one that is a supermarket's own version of the brand. Are the group able to work out which is the original?

Draw out the fact that many Christians struggle to know what God wants them to do or whether what they feel they should be doing is coming from God or from themselves. Working this out is part of the Christian journey.

 Step further

- Have you ever heard or felt God calling you? Would you like to?
- How would you feel if you were called by God to do something specific?
- Do you think it is easy to respond to God's call? Why or why not?

Spend some time praying with your group. You could use words, just focus quietly on a candle or have some appropriate music playing in the background. It is an opportunity to be still and listen to God.

Challenge for the week

Spend some time this week talking and listening to God.

Session 6

Serving God and others

Planning sheet

Reminder...	
What preparations do you need to make for the room, refreshments, and so on?	

Prayer	
When and how will you pray during this session? (See ideas for creative prayer on page 66 for help.)	

Introductory activity

Activity option	Time allocated	Equipment and materials

God

Activity option	Time allocated	Equipment and materials

Others

Activity option	Time allocated	Equipment and materials

Me

Activity option	Time allocated	Equipment and materials

Total time allocated _____

Reflection on the session

- How did the group respond to the activities?

- What went well?

- Did the timings work?

- What needs to be reinforced in the next session?

- What was learnt that will be useful for planning in the future?

- If the session is to be run over two weeks, what material was covered and what still needs to be covered? (Make a note.)

- What else has the content of this session made you think about?

Session 6

Serving God and others

Programme

This session explores vocation in the context of serving through volunteering. It will ask the young people to think about their gifts and skills, leading them towards deciding in Session 7 what they would like to do for their placement.

Recap

Ask the group what they can remember about the last session. What did they discover about God and themselves?

Journal

Invite the young people to share what they thought about when writing up their journal.

NB: It is important to make it clear that this is entirely voluntary and that the journal is private unless people feel comfortable sharing parts of it.

Introductory activity

The aim of the activities below is to explore the meaning of service in a wide context. Choose the option that is most appropriate for your group.

Option One

Invite the group to line up at one end of the room. The object of the game is to travel from one end of the room to the other, taking one step for each word association. The activity finishes when someone reaches the opposite side of the room. The group leader calls out a word, and the participants can move one step for each word they can call out, associated with the first word. For example, if the leader shouts out the word 'God', associated words could be 'omnipotent', 'Lord', 'Saviour', 'powerful' and so on. In this example, if one person shouted out these four words, they could take four steps forward.

Suggested lead words are: serve; follow; God; share; commitment; caring; giving; stewardship; skills; gifts; unconditional; friend; teacher; leader; team; individual; other.

Option Two

Photocopy the 'Would you or wouldn't you?' cards on page 85 or download the page from the website www.barnabasinchurches.org.uk/extra-resources/. Cut out the separate tasks and place them upside down on a table. Invite the group to take turns to pick one, then ask the question, 'Would you or wouldn't you do this task?' The young people answer honestly 'yes' or 'no'. After the activity, reflect on their response by exploring whether it was harder to say 'yes' or 'no'. What helped them to make their decisions?

Option Three

Ask the group to make two circles, one inside the other. The two circles walk in opposite directions as music is being played. As soon as the music stops, the circles face each other and the 'pairs' name one thing they would like to learn to do. Repeat the circular movement twice more, each time stopping to tell each other the following: an existing hobby that they enjoy, and one thing that they don't like doing.

God

Choose the option below that is most appropriate for your group.

Option One

Have available some pictures of the apostle Paul, a map of Greece, a selection of Bibles, pictures of how people would have dressed in the first century AD, and a selection of food from Greece (such as feta cheese, flat bread, olives, tzatziki, and so on).

While the group members are trying the foods and looking at the pictures, share a little bit about Corinth.

Begin by explaining that Corinth was an important city in biblical times. It was on a very narrow section of land (called an 'isthmus') in the southern part of Greece. It was the capital city of the region called Achaia. It had two harbours and, because it was a busy centre for trade, Corinth was a good place for the gospel to spread. Merchants and travellers would hear the message and take it with them when they moved on. There were many different people in Corinth. There were Romans, because it was a Roman colony. (A colony is a city or country that another country controls.) There were also Greeks, Jews and people from Asia and from further east. There were wealthy people and many slaves.

Read the following Bible passage.

What you are doing is much more than a service that supplies God's people with what they need. It is something that will make many others thank God… You believed the message about Christ, and you obeyed it by sharing generously with God's people and with everyone else.

2 CORINTHIANS 9:12–13

Jesus spent most of his ministry providing service to others and modelling discipleship. Part of being a disciple is about offering service to others, enabling God to reach out to others through us.

Draw a large outline of a person on unpasted lining wallpaper or flipchart paper. On the inside of the body, write all the individual needs that we have, if we are to survive, develop and prosper as a person in our communities. Round the outside of the body outline, write who can meet those needs for us in our church and community.

Draw out the fact that we can't meet all our needs on our own. We need to support and help each other through service. If we give our time freely to help and serve in our communities, others will be encouraged to do the same.

Option Two

The Bible teaches that God's Holy Spirit gives us talents and gifts to use in God's service. Yet sometimes those gifts seem to work against our natural inclinations. Invite the group to look up the following Bible stories. You might like to use different Bible versions.

- Moses is asked to lead God's people out of Egypt (Exodus 3:1–12; 4:10–16).
- David the shepherd-boy is made king (1 Samuel 16:1–13).
- Jesus chooses his first disciples (Luke 5:1–11).

Bring out the following points from the stories.

- Moses said that he had never been a good speaker, but God gave him the ability and strength to carry out the role he was called to do.
- God chose a small shepherd-boy to defeat a mighty warrior; he also gave David the qualities to be a king.

- God transformed Jesus' first disciples from simple fishermen into leaders who began the Christian church and left their mark on the course of history.

Talk together about how God can use us, even when we are out of our comfort zones, by giving us gifts we wouldn't have thought we could have. Talk together about the gifts that God gave to Moses, David and Jesus' first disciples, and then explore the gifts that God may want to give to us. What examples can the group think of? How might we use these gifts? How do we recognise God's gifts in us and in others?

Option Three

Beforehand, prepare a game of pass-the-parcel. In each layer of the parcel wrapping, place a piece of paper with one of the gifts from the list below written on it. (You may choose to add to the list provided, to make it more appropriate for your group.) Write the words of 1 Corinthians 12:4–6 on a piece of paper and wrap the paper around it a small mirror. Place the mirror at the centre of the parcel.

There are different kinds of spiritual gifts, but they all come from the same Spirit. There are different ways to serve the same Lord, and we can each do different things. Yet the same God works in all of us and helps us in everything we do.

1 CORINTHIANS 12:4–6

As the young people unwrap each layer, talk about the gift that is revealed. Who might have the gift? Is the gift something that can be learnt? How might the gift be shared with others? When the final layer is reached, encourage the person who opened it to read out the verse and then pass the mirror round to each person. As the mirror is passed round, encourage everyone to look in the mirror and think about their gifts.

God-given gifts include being good at:

- Encouraging others
- Public speaking
- Singing
- DIY skills
- Being patient
- Speaking to people
- Teaching
- Being a good listener
- Being kind
- Being gentle
- Making people laugh
- Creativity and artistic skills
- Fixing things
- Reading

- Writing poetry
- Being supportive
- Being a good friend

Others

This section explores the different kinds of service that people give in their communities. Choose the option below that is most appropriate for your group.

Option One

You will need a selection of local and national newspapers, sheets of flipchart paper and glue.

Divide the group into teams and give each team a selection of the newspapers, a sheet of flipchart paper and some glue. Ask everyone to spread the newspapers out in front of them. The object of the activity is to find articles relating to people who serve in their communities. When they find an article, they should tear it out and read it to their group, then stick it to the flipchart paper. When everyone has finished, take some time for each of the teams to share the articles they found with the rest of the group.

Use the questions below to begin a discussion.

- What did you like about the articles?
- What, if anything, particularly stood out for you?
- What, if anything, did you read that inspired you to do something similar?

The flipchart sheets could be used at the end of the session to help you pray for the people in the articles.

Option Two

Beforehand, download from the internet a selection of stories about people who have made a difference in society or have served others in some way. The website www.bbc.co.uk/history/historic_figures is a useful resource for stories of people such as William Wilberforce and Marie Curie. (As an alternative, you could use the biographies of biblical characters such as Paul, Simon Peter, Mary the mother of Jesus, David, Martha and Mary of Bethany or, indeed, Jesus.) Cut up the biographies into separate cards and place them in a hat or small box.

Split the group into pairs. One person in each pair takes the role of the interviewer and the other takes the role of the interviewee. Ask the interviewee to pick one of the biographies out of the hat and allow everyone time to read through the story of the person they or their partner has picked. Encourage the group to get into character. Give the interviewers a few moments to

think of some questions to ask the interviewee. In their pairs, the interviewers then question the interviewees. When they have finished, invite each pair to feed back to the group what they have discovered about the person they drew out of the hat.

Option Three

Invite to the session some people in your church or local community who are involved in roles that serve others or who are fulfilling a vocation. Make sure they know that they will be required to share for three minutes about their role and vocation and that the group will be asking them questions.

Before the visitors arrive, ask the group to write three questions that they would like to ask the guests about their role or vocation. If they wish, the young people can ask further questions that occur to them during the session. Invite everyone to sit in a circle, including the guests, and invite each visitor in turn to speak about their role for three minutes. After each person has spoken, give the group an opportunity to ask questions before the next person speaks.

Alternatively, use a speed dating technique by providing chairs for the guests to sit on, spaced around the room at different stations. Place a couple of chairs in front of each guest for the young people to sit on. The group members rotate around the stations, spending three minutes with each guest. Ring a bell or buzzer to indicate that it is time to move round.

Me

This section explores the young people's own skills and interests, helping them to reflect on what they might like to try for their placement. Choose the option below that is most appropriate for your group.

Option One

Photocopy the gifts and skills cards on page 86, or download them from www.barnabasinchurches.org.uk/extra-resources/. Use the cards to prompt discussion about individual gifts. Place the cards face down on the table in four piles: Heart, Abilities, Personality and Experience. Ask everyone to take it in turns to choose a card and read the question to the group. Anyone can answer the question. The questions will help the young people to think about their different gifts.

Option Two

Photocopy the 'Which task?' sheets on pages 87–89 or download them from www.barnabasinchurches.org.

uk/extra-resources/. Give one copy to everyone in the group. Allow everyone time to think about the different tasks and to fill out the sheets. Invite them to draw smiley faces in their answers or, alternatively, supply some smiley face stickers for them to use. They can add further tasks to the sheet as appropriate.

Taking care to be sensitive to the group's feelings, invite everyone to get into pairs to talk about what they have chosen on the sheet. Use the questions below to prompt discussion.

- Did any of your choices surprise you?
- Are there any tasks you haven't chosen that you should have? Why didn't you choose them?
- What interested you most about the tasks on the list?
- Are there tasks you would like to do that are not on the list?
- Is there something that really stands out on the list, that you want to try?

Option Three

The following activity can be carried out individually or in small groups. Using the community survey in the journal, invite the young people to write down all the different roles and responsibilities that there are in your church and local community. Next, draw a circle around each of the roles and, in the circle, write the answers to the following questions.

- What gifts and skills do you think this role requires?
- Does the role require a commitment of time?
- How difficult would it be to do this role?

Encourage the group to think about their own individual gifts and skills and then to choose five roles they would like try. Use the questions below for reflection and discussion.

- How difficult was it to choose five roles or responsibilities?
- What influenced your choices?
- In what ways will your gifts and skills help you carry out your chosen roles or responsibilities?

 **Step further**

Divide the group equally into two. Ask one group to form a tight circle in the centre of the room, facing outwards. Ask the other group to form a looser circle around the inner circle, facing inwards. Use the questions below to help the group reflect on the session. Add further questions as appropriate. Allow a few minutes for the pairs facing each other to discuss one of the questions,

then ask the outer circle to rotate one space clockwise. Ask the next question.

Take as long as is needed to allow everyone the opportunity to have one-on-one discussions with as many different people in the group as possible.

- What have you learnt about yourself in this session?
- How difficult is it to recognise what gifts you have?
- What skills would you like to learn?
- Talk about a time when you used your gifts or skills.
- Think of someone you admire. What gifts do you recognise in him or her?

Finish by emphasising that we all have a variety of gifts and skills, some of which we are naturally good at and some of which we learn and develop with practice. Some gifts we know we have, and some we don't; other people can help us to see those skills and can encourage us to use and develop them.

Challenge for the week

Look carefully to see all the different ways that people serve others in your church and community. See how many ways you can spot!

Try it!

Planning sheet

Reminder...	
What preparations do you need to make for the room, refreshments, and so on?	

Prayer	
When and how will you pray during this session? (See ideas for creative prayer on page 66 for help.)	

Essential preparation for the session

- Ensure that the completed volunteer placement forms have been returned to you in readiness for the 'Try it!' exercise. These can be found on page 62.
- Invite some of the placement volunteers to the session to talk about their role and to respond to questions from the young people.
- Remember to ask the young people to bring their journals to the session.
- Remind yourself of what has been covered over the previous six sessions.

The session

Section	Time allocated	Equipment and materials
Introductory activity		
Making choices		
Placements		
God		
Recap		

Follow-up

- Ensure that all those offering placements have a copy of the guidelines on page 63.
- Ensure that the young people have completed the placement details in their journals.
- Ensure that everyone has completed an evaluation form (including all the leaders). See pages 64 and 65.
- Arrange for the completed evaluation forms to be available for the next meeting of your church leadership team.
- Arrange for the whole church to receive feedback.

Total time allocated _____

Reflection on the session

- How did the group respond to the activities?

- What went well?

- What do you need to do to run future Participate! programmes?

- What else has the content of this session made you think about?

52

Try it!

Programme

This session is intended to prepare the group for their placements and, for this reason, is laid out differently from the previous sessions. Instead of activity options, the sections are designed to be used in their entirety.

Recap

Ask the group to think about anything they have discovered during Participate! that has surprised them. What have they discovered about God and themselves?

Journal

Invite the young people to share what they thought about when writing up their journal.

NB: It is important to make it clear that this is entirely voluntary and that the journal is private unless people feel comfortable sharing parts of it.

Introductory activity

Explain that this final session is about exploring what everyone would like to try, based on the different roles and skills they identified in the previous session. It is also about exploring the possibility of learning new skills. It is an opportunity to volunteer to get involved either in church-based activities or in the wider community. Explain that everyone will be working alongside someone in the church or community who has already volunteered to be involved in a particular role. It will be an opportunity for sharing experience and learning together. The exercise is designed to help the young people grow in confidence and to enhance existing skills or learn new skills together.

You will need a roll of lining wallpaper, pens, sticky notes and a small basket. The young people will need to have their journals with them.

Draw a winding path on the paper, making the path at least eight feet long if you have the space. Mark six signposts on the path, each labelled with the title of one of the first six Participate! sessions. Put the pens and sticky notes in a basket. Write the prompt questions below along the top of the sheet.

- What do you remember about the session?
- What was your favourite part of the session?
- What did you learn from the session?

Using the session aims as a prompt (marked as 'Programme' at the head of each session), remind the group about the previous six sessions. Hand out the pens and sticky notes. Invite the group to take some time at each of the signposts to write something on the sticky notes about each session. Encourage the young people to use their journals to remind them of what they have covered.

When they have finished, invite the young people to walk along the path and reflect on the things they have written down. Prompt questions for reflection could include the following.

- What stands out for you about this journey?
- What was the easiest part of the journey so far?
- What was the hardest part of the journey so far?
- What expectations do you have for the next stage of the journey?
- What makes you apprehensive about the next stage of the journey?

Making choices

In preparation for this section, have available the volunteer placement forms. You might want to invite some of the people who have volunteered to help with 'Try it!' placements to come along to the session, to chat to the young people and answer questions or to share briefly about their role.

Photocopy the question sheet on page 90 or download it from the website www.barnabasinchurches. org.uk/extra-resources/. Give each person a copy of the sheet and ask them to find people in the group who can answer the questions. Give prizes for the first person to complete the sheet, the person with the most names (you can have more than one name next to an item), and the last one to complete the sheet.

Take some time with the group to look through and complete the Session 7 material in their journals. Give the group an opportunity to ask questions about the 'Try it!' placements and to share what they have written in their journals if they want to. Encourage the group to continue to use the journal during the coming weeks for reflection.

Next, display the volunteer placement forms in a prominent place and invite the group to take time to look at them. Make sticky notes available for everyone to write down questions they may want to ask. Create a space on the wall for the young people to place their completed sticky notes.

If you have invited people into the session, invite them to talk about their roles. Give the group the opportunity to ask questions. You may want the role holders to stay throughout the session.

Look at the sticky notes together and answer the questions that have arisen.

Placements

When everyone has had the opportunity to look at the possible placements and ask any questions, invite the young people to choose one they would like to try. Once they have made their choice, complete the box at the bottom of the volunteer placement form. Ask everyone also to write their placement details down on page 45 of their journals. Complete the young person's details on the placement guideline sheet and pass this to the role holder.

Take time to answer any further questions from the group.

God

Photocopy the Bible passage below and stick it on to a piece of card (one for each person in the group). At the end of the session, give everyone a copy and suggest that they might like to keep it with them as they prepare for and carry out their placements.

No test or temptation that comes your way is beyond the course of what others have had to face. All you need to remember is that God will never let you down; he'll never let you be pushed past your limit; he'll always be there to help you come through it.

1 CORINTHIANS 10:13 (*The Message*)

Recap

Give everyone a blank piece of paper and ask them to draw the outline of a house. Underneath the house (where the foundations are), invite them to write all the things they have learnt about God over the last six sessions. Invite them to think of a Bible passage used in one of the sessions that could become a part of the foundations of their house. Inside the house, ask them to write or draw all the things they are good at, what they like doing, all the skills they have and hope to learn through their 'Try it!' placements, and also the hopes they might have for how they will serve in the future. Remind the young people that God and his teachings are the foundation that their lives are to be built upon.

Use one of the prayer suggestions on page 66 to close the session.

Appendix
One

Step-by-step flow chart

Step 1

- Obtain the agreement of the leadership of the church and the young people to undertake Participate! (This could be discussed at a specific meeting, over a meal together.)
- Make sure young people and the church community are aware of what is involved.

Step 8

- Monitor and evaluate the impact of Participate! and develop ways to continue.

Step 2

- Think of possible ways to get the whole church involved (for example, announce at Sunday service, use commitment sheets, housegroup, prayer group, and so on).

Step 7

- Deliver the session that prepares the group for their chosen 'Try it!' placement.
- Arrange the details of the placements with the group and with the church members who have volunteered to help.
- Oversee the young people for the duration of the placement.

Step 3

- Decide when the sessions will run (for example, Sunday mornings, midweek club, start a specific group, and so on) and where you will meet.
- Decide when the 'Try it!' placements will take place and for how long.

Step 6

- Create opportunities for sharing with the rest of the church as you go through the Participate! programme (for example, using newsletter, website, Sunday services, and so on).

Step 5

- Take time to think about each session. Use the planning sheet as a guide to delivery.
- Reflect after each session.
- Encourage the group to use their journals between each session.

Step 4

- Encourage church members to complete and return volunteer placement forms so that you will be able to identify church members who are willing to have a young person working alongside them for the duration of the 'Try it!' placement. (Please refer to your church's safeguarding policy.)

 Reproduced with permission from *Participate!* published by BRF 2012 (978 1 84101 854 6) www.barnabasinchurches.org.uk

Reflecting on children's ministry

For the programme to work well, the church as a whole needs to understand the theology that underpins the resource, and the responsibility—both collectively and individually—that church members have for the young people in the church. This chapter is designed to help you think theologically and practically about children's ministry and the contribution that the Participate! programme could offer. You could use this material as an individual, as part of a leadership team or in a house group session. The chapter is also available as a download from the website www.barnabasinchurches.org.uk/extra-resources/. Read through the material and use the questions to stimulate reflection and discussion.

Bread and fish for all

After this, Jesus went across the Sea of Galilee (some call it Tiberias). A huge crowd followed him, attracted by the miracles they had seen him do among the sick. When he got to the other side, he climbed a hill and sat down, surrounded by his disciples. It was nearly time for the Feast of Passover, kept annually by the Jews.

When Jesus looked out and saw that a large crowd had arrived, he said to Philip, 'Where can we buy bread to feed these people?' He said this to stretch Philip's faith. He already knew what he was going to do.

Philip answered, 'Two hundred silver pieces wouldn't be enough to buy bread for each person to get a piece.'

One of the disciples—it was Andrew, brother to Simon Peter—said, 'There's a little boy here who has five barley loaves and two fish. But that's a drop in the bucket for a crowd like this.'

Jesus said, 'Make the people sit down.' There was a nice carpet of green grass in this place. They sat down, about five thousand of them. Then Jesus took the bread and, having given thanks, gave it to those who were seated. He did the same with the fish. All ate as much as they wanted.

When the people had eaten their fill, he said to his disciples, 'Gather the leftovers so nothing is wasted.' They went to work and filled twelve large baskets with leftovers from the five barley loaves.

The people realised that God was at work among them in what Jesus had just done.

JOHN 6:1–15 (*THE MESSAGE*)

In the Bible, the story of the feeding of the five thousand appears in each of the four Gospels: Matthew, Mark, Luke and John. The accounts by Matthew, Mark and Luke are very similar to each other; John's account is the only one in which the five loaves of barley and two small fish are given to Jesus by a young boy.

Questions for reflection and discussion

- Why do you think only one Gospel mentions that the food was given by a child?
- Read the accounts in the other three Gospels (Matthew 14:13–21; Mark 6:30–44; Luke 9:12–17). What other aspects strike you from these accounts?

The New Testament reveals much about Jesus' life. The insight in John's account of the feeding of the five thousand helps us to appreciate Jesus' views about children and young people and, combined with an understanding of his teaching in this respect, provides the foundation on which ministry with children and young people should be based.

2. Participating in a faith community: Young people need to experience what it means to serve as well as to be served; this is how their faith will become living and life-influencing.
3. Modelling on people in the faith community: People in leadership roles have an influence over the lives of young people. If young people consider them to have honesty and integrity in the way they share their faith and live their lives, they will identify with them and emulate them.
4. Instruction in the word of God: The Bible needs to be an integral part of everyday living. It is important to understand its context, to explore the multiple messages it may convey and to be able to apply it to everyday living.
5. Opportunities for responsible choices: Young people need opportunities to practise their faith in a safe and supportive environment, and to question and challenge without fear of rejection or rebuke.

The Participate! programme is based on these five processes of faith development. It is a challenging approach, which requires a commitment from the church community, church workers and the young people themselves.

Questions for reflection and discussion

- Think about the five ways of developing faith. Do you recognise any of them in your own journey of faith?
- Which of the five ways is seen currently in the children's and youth ministry at your church?

Participate! enables young people to explore vocation and calling, to discover how they can serve God and others today. Allowing opportunities for this to happen is an important part of children's and youth ministry.

Questions for reflection and discussion

- Who or what has helped (or helps) you to explore your calling?
- How easy is it for you to exercise your vocation in your current situation?
- How does the idea of being called by God make you feel?

Think about your church's ministry with children and young people.

- Who is it trying to reach?
- What is its purpose?
- How can your whole church become more involved in the children's and youth ministry that is taking place (or could take place)?
- How can you personally make a difference to the discipleship journey of the children and young people at your church and in your community?

In the light of the above, if your church has a catechism or a statement of faith, do you know what it is and why the church feels it is necessary? Do you think it works for the 21st century? What questions and answers stand out for you? What might you change, and why?

Finally, read through the information about the Participate! programme. You may need to re-read or photocopy the three paragraphs headed 'What is Participate?', 'Why explore vocation with 9–14s?' and 'Practicalities' on page 8, which explain the basis for the programme. In what ways could you as an individual and as a whole church be involved in the programme? How could you make the programme sustainable so that it is not just a one-off experience?

Bible texts that support our understanding of Jesus' attitude towards children include the following.

The Word became a human being and lived here with us (John 1:14).

Let the children come to me! Don't try to stop them. People who are like these little children belong to the kingdom of God (Mark 10:14).

'I promise you this. If you don't change and become like a child, you will never get into the kingdom of heaven' (Matthew 18:3).

'It will be terrible for people who cause even one of my little followers to sin. Those people would be better off thrown into the deepest part of the ocean with a heavy stone tied around their necks!' (Matthew 18:6).

Through these verses we recognise that:

- Jesus didn't enter the world as an adult but as a baby. He had first-hand experience of the life of a child at that time, and he knew the pressure and fears that they face.
- Jesus valued children and young people. He believed that, no matter what their age or ability, they had gifts that he could use for the benefit of others.
- Jesus believed it was the responsibility of the community of believers to enable children and young people to encounter God.
- Jesus knew that life for a child or young person is hard. He directed adults to keep young people safe and to nurture them on their spiritual journey.

Questions for reflection and discussion

- What are your thoughts about Jesus' attitude towards children?

For many churches, the Sunday school environment is the main focal point for teaching children and young people about the Christian faith. When Robert Raikes initiated the Sunday school movement in 1780, some people regarded Sunday schools as an early form of evangelism; some suggested that they were about the indoctrination of children, while others believed them to be about the mass education of the working classes, which (they thought) could ultimately threaten the hierarchy of Britain.

Sunday school lessons consisted of instruction on the Bible and the catechism—an uncomplicated book in the form of questions and answers, containing a summary of the principles of the Christian faith maintained by a particular church. Sunday schools were evangelistic in the sense that, through Christian education, children and young people were expected to experience an encounter with God and become part of the Christian faith.

Christians have different points of view about Christian education, its purpose, the theology (thoughts and beliefs about God) that underpin it, and how it should be delivered. These views shape the way we hear God's story and share it.

Questions for reflection and discussion

- What are your memories of your time in Sunday school or of the way your faith was taught through school?
- When and where did you learn the most about your faith? Was it when you were a child?
- When were you the most interested in the Christian faith?
- What do you think the purpose of Christian education should be?

Many people, like those who started the early Sunday schools, believe that we hear God's story only through the Bible and church traditions. Others, however, believe that personal experience and reason (what is reasonable or logical or makes sense based on our scientific understanding) influence the way God's story is heard and understood.

If we do not hold these theological influences—scripture, tradition, personal experience and reason—in balance, we end up not fully understanding God's story and not presenting it in a way that makes sense. We also restrict the way we live our Christian lives.

Some churches assume that, in order to pass Christian traditions and faith between generations in a consistent way, the methods used must remain the same. This ignores the fact that society has changed, that there are now many subcultures and that people learn in different ways.

Questions for reflection and discussion

- How has society changed since you were a child?

Christian ministry with children and young people must enable a connection with God, the world and each other, so that young people can think as disciples, talk as disciples and be disciples.

Nowadays, the accounts of many churches, Sunday school workers, children and young people suggest that this connection is achieved with varying degrees of success.

Questions for reflection and discussion

- Why do you think churches are successful or unsuccessful in their ministry with young people?

Although church attendance is declining, there is an anomaly in that many children and young people are baptised (or dedicated). At these services, members of each Christian community make promises to the child, to help him or her grow in faith and in the knowledge and love of God.

Questions for reflection and discussion

- Why do you think so many people unconnected with the church want their children to be baptised?
- What can the church do to offer ongoing support to families who seek baptism for their children?

The Christian nurture of children and young people is the responsibility of the whole church. Jesus emphasises this in his teaching. Faith development in young people is extremely important; it requires an integrated approach and the emphasis should be on Christian nurture and growth.

Living as a disciple requires a commitment to worship, prayer, discipline and service. It involves reflecting on God through the influences of the Bible, tradition, experience and reason.

Questions for reflection and discussion

- Which of these four do you find the most useful in your own faith development, and why?

The Christian faith cannot be learnt. Churches need to direct their ministry so that young people can grow as disciples with a balanced approach to theology and within a Christian community that values, understands and affirms them. The American author and speaker Lawrence O. Richards suggests the following five processes for faith development.

1. Belonging to a faith community: Young people need to feel as if they are a part of an authentic faith community that models the messages they are given, helping them to give and receive love, which is essential to developing faith.

Commitment to Participate!

Church members

What is Participate?

The Participate! programme has six sessions designed to give young people the opportunity to explore and discuss various issues, to get them thinking about themselves as individuals and what involvement God wants them to have in the church and community. At the end of the six sessions, the young people will get the chance to take part in roles in the community or church. In doing so, they will begin to explore their gifts and talents and how these can be used to help the community or church.

The role of individual church members is as follows.

- Pray…
  - that the young people will make connections between the material they are exploring and their own lives.
  - for the group leaders and facilitators.
  - for your own journey as a disciple.
  - for the church to be open to the direction in which God is leading the young people.

- Tell others your story
  - Think about your story. How did you get to this place, who were your influences, and what were your struggles?
  - Think about the best way to tell your story.

- Discover the young people's stories
  - Listen to stories of the young people's spiritual journeys and everyday lives.

- Be involved
  - Offer to be involved with the placements by allowing a young person to experience your role in the church or community.
  - Think about the possibility of letting a young person shadow you in your professional workplace.
  - Think about the possibility of involving a young person in your voluntary role at church or in the community.

The role of the church as a whole is as follows.

- Pray as a church for the young people and those who are working with them.
- Think about the themes that the young people are discussing on the Participate! programme. (This could be as part of Sunday worship, in house groups, and so on.)
- Make space for young people to be part of the full life of the church by offering continued opportunities to explore and develop vocation and discipleship.

Signed   _____

Date   _____

(Please sign your name as a mark of your commitment.)

Commitment to Participate!

Group leaders and facilitators

What is Participate?

The Participate! programme has six sessions designed to give young people the opportunity to explore and discuss various issues, to get them thinking about themselves as individuals and what involvement God wants them to have in the church and community. At the end of the six sessions, the young people will get the chance to take part in roles in the community or church. In doing so, they will begin to explore their gifts and talents and how these can be used to help the community or church.

Your role as a group leader or facilitator is as follows.

- Value and pray for all members of the group.

- Create a safe and welcoming environment.

- Work with and explore together with the young people.

- Encourage involvement of all members of the group.

- Be open and encouraging of questions; don't expect to have all the answers.

- Be sensitive to different learning styles and abilities.

- Take time to think about how you will facilitate each of the sessions.

- Help the young people to plan their chosen placements.

- Be willing to share your own story of faith.

- Together with the young people, share your experiences of Participate! with the rest of the church community.

Signed _____

Date   _____

(Please sign your name as a mark of your commitment.)

Commitment to Participate!

Young people

What is Participate?

The Participate! programme has six sessions designed to give you the opportunity to spend time exploring and discussing issues. It aims to get you thinking about yourself and what involvement God wants you to have in the church and community. At the end of the six sessions, you will get the chance to take part in roles in your community or church in a way that you may never have tried before. In doing so, you will begin to explore your gifts and talents and how you can use them to help your community or church.

Your role is as follows:

- Be welcoming to everyone in your group.

- Allow everyone the chance to speak.

- Pray for each other.

- Be willing to try new things.

- Share your experience of Participate! with members of the church.

- Use your journal to record your thoughts and feelings about the sessions.

Signed _____

Date _____

(Please sign your name as a mark of your commitment.)

Volunteer placement form

Please hand the completed form to the Participate! group leader named below.

Participate group leader: _____

Name of role holder: _____

Name of role: _____

Description of duties: _____

List of skills needed to carry out the role: _____

Previous experience for carrying out the role: _____

New skills learnt for the role: _____

Role holder's story

Why do you do this role? _____

How did you become involved? _____

What motivated you to volunteer? _____

Practical requirements

Day and time when the role is carried out: _____

Frequency of role: _____

Location of role: _____

The following section is to be completed during Participate! Session 7 by the group leader.

Name of young person carrying out the placement: _____

Name of role: _____

Name of role holder: _____

Day and time of placement: _____

Placement location: _____ Placement date: _____

Placement guidelines

NB: This sheet should be handed to the placement role holders when details of the young person's involvement have been finalised and written below.

Rationale

The purpose of 'Try it!' is to offer young people an understanding of the opportunities available for serving in their church and community. During their placement, they should be encouraged to enhance their existing skills, learn new skills and share skills as they grow in confidence. The experience can help young people to grow in Christian discipleship and learn how to be effective contributors in their church, community and society. It should be a two-way experience, giving both the role holder and the young person an opportunity to learn together.

Practicalities

The young person will have the volunteer placement form that you completed, outlining your role. They should be given meaningful tasks to undertake and should be able to identify how their input fits into the wider church or community. Please ensure that you have read and are familiar with your church policy and guidelines on safeguarding and working with children and young people. Please also ensure that you do not work with the young person solely on a one-to-one basis and that other people are present when the young person is carrying out their placement.

The young person should be given feedback. They will benefit from constructive and helpful feedback, and the church will benefit from hearing the young person's views about their placement experience.

The young person should receive an introductory briefing about the role and be given the opportunity to familiarise themselves with the role before commencing the placement. The opportunity should be given for the young person to ask questions and to go through the placement description with you as the accompanying adult.

Evaluation

The hope is that the placement opportunity will enrich the mission and ministry of the church and community and enable all those involved to grow and progress on their discipleship journey. Evaluation is an essential part of this experience and you will be provided with an evaluation sheet to complete after the placement has ended.

Top tips for working alongside young people

- Try to understand how young people communicate and keep the use of jargon to a minimum. Use eye contact and be attentive to what the young person has to say.
- Ask the young person what they think. Do not presume to know what young people are thinking or feeling: ask them. If you don't understand at first, ask them to repeat what they have said. It is better to ask for confirmation than fail to respond through lack of understanding.
- Give the young person some responsibility, and prevent 'tokenism' by allowing them to have a sense of ownership and control. It is important for them to play an equal role in decision-making.
- Be patient and listen. Don't presume you know what a young person wants to say before they have said it. Wait for them to finish speaking before making comments.

Young person's name: _____

Type of placement: _____

Start date: _____

Start time: _____

Finish date: _____

Finish time: _____

Participate! evaluation form

Group leaders and young people

Please circle whether you are:

A group leader / a young person

Using the scale 1–5, circle the number you feel best answers the question, with one equalling 'No, not at all' and five equalling 'Yes, definitely'. Please include further information in the spaces provided if you wish.

Has Participate! been a positive experience for you?

1   2   3   4   5

Which parts were the most interesting, most useful or most enjoyable?

Do you think that the whole church got involved in Participate?

1   2   3   4   5

How could the church have become more involved?

Did you learn anything from Participate?

1   2   3   4   5

What did you learn?

Did you find organising / taking part in the placement a positive experience?

1   2   3   4   5

What was particularly good or difficult?

Should Participate! be repeated in the future?

1   2   3   4   5

How could it be improved?

 Reproduced with permission from *Participate!* published by BRF 2012 (978 1 84101 854 6) www.barnabasinchurches.org.uk

Placement evaluation form

Role holders

Thank you for your support in enabling a young person to experience your role as a volunteer in the church. So that we can fully assess the success of Participate!, please respond to the questions below about your experience. Your comments will be fed back to the church leadership team to help in the planning and development of work in the church with children and young people.

Using the scale 1–5, circle the number you feel best answers the question, with one equalling 'No, not at all' and five equalling 'Yes, definitely'. Please include further information in the spaces provided if you wish.

Did you feel well prepared to support a young person during the placement?

1   2   3   4   5

Please give details below if you wish.

Did you feel that the exercise was well supported by the whole church?

1   2   3   4   5

Please give details below if you wish.

Did you learn anything from the experience?

1   2   3   4   5

Please give details below if you wish.

In your opinion, was the experience useful for the young person?

1   2   3   4   5

Please give details below if you wish.

Did you enjoy the experience?

1   2   3   4   5

Please give details below if you wish.

If the church was to run Participate! again, what changes would improve it? Please give details below.

Ideas for creative prayer

The following ideas can be used to mix and match ways to pray during the seven sessions. Alternatively, a single idea can be used as an overriding theme for all of the sessions.

Graffiti prayers

Create a prayer wall by covering a surface with lining wallpaper. Suggest that, during the prayer time, the group may write or draw on the wall anything that they want to offer to God in prayer. If the graffiti wall is to be used throughout the programme, factor in time for the group to use it in each session.

Prayer covenant

On A5 cards, write the names of all the people who hold a role in the church and all the young people in the group. Photocopy and distribute these cards to the group and the rest of the church. Ask all those who take the list to commit to praying for all the participants for the next six weeks.

Planting seeds

The following idea can be used as a whole-church activity or just with the group.

Place a large tub (or tubs) of earth where everyone can see it. Alternatively, use seed trays. Give everyone a seed or bulb to represent the wealth of skills and gifts that God has placed in each one of us. Use the activity as a focal point to encourage everyone to pray about their gifts and skills.

Balloon prayers

Write or draw prayers on small pieces of paper and place each prayer into a balloon. Fill the balloons with air and tie the ends. Take the balloons into your church garden or any open space and release them into the air. Alternatively, tie a piece of string the length of the room just above head height and tie the prayer balloons along the line. If the prayer balloons are to be used throughout the programme, add more balloons each week. Over the course of the six sessions, the group may want to pop some of the balloons and re-read the prayers.

Catalyst prayers

Create a prayer area using several displays or activities that will help the group to pray. Write the wording on cards and set the card beside the visual aid.

- Display a clock, stopwatch or timer. Wording: 'How much time do we give to God? How do we use the time that God has given us?'
- Have available a basket of pebbles and a cross. Wording: 'What things are we nervous or worried about? Take a pebble to represent those things and place it at the foot of the cross.'
- Set up a bowl of water. Wording: 'We need water to live. It makes things grow; it cleanses and refreshes us. Dip your fingers into the water. How do we use water?'

Carry out the activity as indicated and think about the questions. Write or draw a prayer on a sticky note and stick it on to a prayer board in the prayer area.

God's story; my story

Each one of us is unique, made individually by God. Each one of us has a story. Cut sheets of A4 paper lengthwise into four strips. Invite the group to write or draw about themselves on a strip. Fasten the strips to make a paper chain, and hang it around the room or in church. If you wish to add to the chain throughout the programme, during each session ask the group to write something about their experience of each session—what they have learnt and what their hopes are.

String of beads

Beads have been used as an aid to prayer for centuries. Take a length of thick thread and some beads of different colours. Tie the beads on to the thread to represent different areas of life, such as faith, family, friends, school, hobbies and so on. Use the different colours to mark the different areas or events. Use the beads to help you pray about the different areas of life.

Learning styles

It is widely accepted that not everyone learns in exactly the same way. We will all have preferred styles in which we learn best. Too often, in our work with children and young people, we focus on a limited number of styles of learning, and this can disengage the young people we are trying to reach. It is important therefore that we begin to understand what is meant by 'learning styles'.

There has been much research undertaken in this field. Howard Gardner's Multiple Intelligences theory outlines seven different types of intelligences and how people with these intelligences prefer to learn:

- **Linguistic**: prefers words and language; learns best with speech, reading and writing.
- **Logical/mathematical**: prefers to learn with logic, numbers and reasoning.
- **Musical**: prefers to learn with music, sound and rhythm.
- **Bodily/kinaesthetic**: prefers to learn when it involves movement and action.
- **Spatial-visual**: prefers to learn with pictures and images.
- **Interpersonal**: prefers to learn in groups; likes to hear about other people's feelings.
- **Intrapersonal**: prefers to learn alone; likes self study and is self-aware.

Gardner suggests that most people are strong in three of the above intelligences. This would indicate that we should constantly vary our approaches to enable children and young people to engage and learn in accessible ways that link with their particular capabilities and interests.

Another simple way to remember and understand different learning styles is the VAK model. You will see an overlap here with Gardner's theory.

- Visual
- Auditory
- Kinesthetic

Visual learners like seeing and reading. They will prefer tasks to do with pictures, diagrams, films, displays, written handouts and books. Auditory learners like listening and speaking and will prefer tasks centred on discussion, sounds and music. 'Kinesthetic' comes from the Greek words for 'move' and 'sensation'. Kinesthetic learners prefer touching, feeling, doing and moving and will engage in practical activities.

When planning activities and tasks for children and young people, it is useful to think through the learning styles to make sure that you include a variety and are not too focused on one particular style. Even though people may have a preferred learning style, it would be incorrect to limit them to just that way of learning. However, if you are struggling to engage young people with what you are doing in your group, it may be worth considering whether a different approach that connects with a different learning style might encourage greater involvement.

Throughout the sessions in Participate! we have included a variety of activities that complement the different learning styles, so you should be able to engage and challenge all types of learner.

If you are interested in finding out more about learning styles, there are many online sites where you can discover your own learning style.

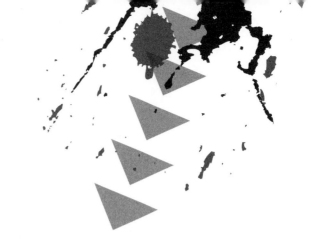

Appendix Two

Worksheets for the sessions

People match

If you find someone who fits one of the following descriptions, write their name in the box.

Find someone who...

Has a red toothbrush	Rides a bike to school
Likes pickled onions	Has more than six cousins
Thinks football is boring	Has been camping
Is grumpy in the mornings	Likes PE
Supports a football team	Went abroad last summer
Is frightened of spiders	Plays for a sports team
Has read all the Harry Potter books	Can play chess
Is a vegetarian	Has ever dyed their hair
Has broken an arm or leg	Has been to McDonalds in the last fortnight
Likes to sing	Has wallpaper on their bedroom walls
Likes *Doctor Who*	Can play a musical instrument
Has been skiing	Has ever met anyone famous

My avatar

Choose words from the list below that describe your characteristics. Write the words around the avatar of yourself. Add any extra words that you want. You may want to change the avatar to reflect the words you have chosen.

happy   grumpy   sporty   shy   outgoing   dramatic   thoughtful   lazy   helpful   funny   worried

nervous   friendly   loyal   caring   energetic   musical   artistic   moody   techno-whizz   angry

God's character Bible quotes

In the beginning God created the heavens and the earth. Now the earth was formless and empty, darkness was over the surface of the deep, and the Spirit of God was hovering over the waters. And God said, 'Let there be light,' and there was light. God saw that the light was good.

GENESIS 1:1–4 (NIV)

You are merciful and quick to forgive; you are loving, kind, and very patient.

NEHEMIAH 9:17

For you created my inmost being; you knit me together in my mother's womb. I praise you because I am fearfully and wonderfully made; your works are wonderful, I know that full well. My frame was not hidden from you when I was made in the secret place, when I was woven together in the depths of the earth. Your eyes saw my unformed body; all the days ordained for me were written in your book before one of them came to be. How precious to me are your thoughts, God! How vast is the sum of them!

PSALM 139:13–17 (NIV)

Proclaim the power of God whose majesty is over Israel, whose power is in the heavens. You, God, are awesome in your sanctuary; the God of Israel gives power and strength to his people.

PSALM 68:34–35 (NIV)

Love comes from God, and when we love each other, it shows that we have been given new life. We are now God's children, and we know him. God is love, and anyone who doesn't love others has never known him.

1 JOHN 4:7–8

I waited patiently for the Lord; he turned to me and heard my cry... Many will see and fear the Lord and put their trust in him.

PSALM 40:1, 3 (NIV)

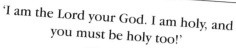

'I am the Lord your God. I am holy, and you must be holy too!'

LEVITICUS 19:2

Shout praises to the Lord! He is good to us, and his love never fails.

PSALM 107:1

The Lord said: I have seen how my people are suffering as slaves in Egypt, and I have heard them beg for my help because of the way they are being mistreated. I feel sorry for them, and I have come down to rescue them from the Egyptians. I will bring my people out of Egypt into a country where there is good land, rich with milk and honey.

EXODUS 3:7–8

God is wise and powerful!

DANIEL 2:20 (GNB)

You rule forever, Lord, and you are on your throne, ready for judgment. You judge the world fairly and treat all nations with justice.

PSALM 9:7–8

God is always honest and fair, and his laws can be trusted. They are true and right and will stand forever.

PSALM 111:7–8

'If you listen to me and do what I tell you, I will be your God, you will be my people, and all will go well for you.'

JEREMIAH 7:23

You are a people holy to the Lord your God. The Lord your God has chosen you out of all the peoples on the face of the earth to be his people, his treasured possession.

DEUTERONOMY 7:6 (NIV)

The Lord is faithful to all his promises and loving toward all he has made.

PSALM 145:13 (NIV 1984)

Made in the image of God

What questions do you have about the idea of being made in the image of God?

What are the positive, good things about being made in God's image?

Write down some of the words that describe God's character.

How does it make you feel when you think of being made in God's image?

What are the difficulties and challenges about being made in God's image?

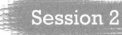

Characteristics grid

Photocopy the grid and cut out the boxes.

helpful	impolite
kind	persevering
outspoken	ambitious
lazy	stubborn
honest	lying
respectful	modest
selfish	humble
rebellious	dedicated
compassionate	jealous
courageous	immature
trustworthy	thoughtful
secretive	arrogant
angry	confident
generous	hard-working
friendly	law-abiding

Cartoon guide to the community of Israel

ADAM and EVE disobey GOD

ADAM and EVE leave the Garden of Eden

NOAH's Ark

God's promise to NOAH

GOD chooses ABRAM

God's promise to ABRAM

ISHMAEL is born

GOD promises ABRAHAM a son

ABRAHAM trusts GOD

ISAAC and REBEKAH have twins

ESAU sells his rights as the firstborn son

ISAAC blesses JACOB

JACOB'S ladder

LEAH and RACHEL

JACOB tricks LABAN

JACOB runs away

JACOB and LABAN make up

JACOB and the ANGEL

JACOB's twelve sons

JOSEPH's dream

JOSEPH is sold as a slave

JOSEPH in prison

 Reproduced with permission from *Participate!* published by BRF 2012 (978 1 84101 854 6) www.barnabasinchurches.org.uk

23 Joseph is made Governor

24 Joseph and his family, reunited

25 The Community of Israel

26 Moses and the burning bush

27 The People escape from Egypt

28 Moses and the 10 Commandments

29 Jesus is born

30 The Christian church grows

'Love your neighbour' scenario cards

There is news on the television about a natural disaster in another part of the world, which has left people homeless and starving. What could you do to be a good neighbour?	In your class at school, you know that there is a person being bullied. The person is not one of your close friends but you are aware of what is happening. What could you do to be a good neighbour?
You know that there is an elderly person living on their own in your street, who doesn't have any family nearby. What could you do to be a good neighbour?	The paper reports that your local hospital will have to shut its children's cancer ward due to lack of funding. What could you do to be a good neighbour?
The local park, where you go regularly, is always covered in litter. What could you do to be a good neighbour?	You are at a bus stop waiting to get home when an elderly woman starts to talk to you. She says that she doesn't get out much and doesn't get much chance to speak to people. What could you do to be a good neighbour?
There has been some gossip going around about one of the girls in your class. Someone tells you the gossip. What could you do to be a good neighbour?	You have noticed that there are quite a lot of homeless people sleeping rough in your area. There are a few who sleep near to your church. What could you do to be a good neighbour?
You notice that your local shop does not stock any Fairtrade chocolate. What could you do to be a good neighbour?	You notice that someone has been posting unpleasant comments about a member of your youth group on Facebook. What could you do to be a good neighbour?
A person in your class has forgotten their lunch and has no money to buy any. What could you do to be a good neighbour?	You were told in church how Christians in China are being treated badly because of their faith. What could you do to be a good neighbour?

The orchestra of Christ

Christ is like an orchestra, which has many musicians;
It is still one orchestra even though it is made up of different instruments.
In the same way, all of us, whether black or white, male or female, young or old, wealthy
or poor, sharp or flat, have been invited to play in concert.

The orchestra is not made up of only one instrument, but of many instruments:
If the drum was to say, 'Because I am not a violin, I don't belong to the orchestra' that
would not keep it from playing its part in the music;
And if the guitar was to say, 'Because I am not a clarinet, I don't belong to the orchestra'
that would not keep it from playing its part in the music.

If the whole orchestra was made up of bagpipes, how could it play rock and roll?
And if the whole orchestra was made up of tambourines, how could it play Beethoven's
Ninth Symphony?
So, the trombone cannot say to the triangle, 'I don't need you!'
Nor can the bassoon say to the banjo, 'I don't need you!'

On the contrary, we cannot do without the parts of the orchestra that seem weaker, and
those instruments which we think aren't worth very much (like the triangles) are the
ones which we treat with greater care.

So, the conductor has put every instrument and musician just where he wants them.
There would not be an orchestra if it were all one harmonica.
As it is, there are many instruments, but one orchestra.

God himself has put the orchestra together so that greater honour is given to those
instruments that need it, like the washboard or Peruvian nose flute,
And so there is no discord in the orchestra but all the musicians play sensitively, listening
to each other.

If one instrument is out of tune, the whole orchestra suffers.
If one instrument plays a beautiful solo, the whole orchestra shares in the ovation.

All of you are Christ's orchestra and each of you has a part to play… in harmony.

'THE ORCHESTRA OF CHRIST' TAKEN FROM *REIGN DANCE: THE WAKING* BY MARTIN JOHN NICHOLLS, PUBLISHED BY THE
FELLOWSHIP OF UNITED REFORMED YOUTH (FURY), 86 TAVISTOCK PLACE, LONDON, WC1H 9RT 1997, ISBN 978 0 85346 167 8.
USED WITH PERMISSION FROM FURY.

Match the story

Moses	Jonah	Peter
He was looking after sheep in the desert and came to Mount Sinai.	God said, 'Go to the great city of Nineveh and say to the people, "The Lord has seen your terrible sins. You are doomed!"'	The disciples got into a boat and started to sail across the lake.
He saw a bush on fire.	The man didn't want to do what God said, so he ran away.	Jesus didn't join them—he went off to pray by himself.
God called to him from the bush.	The man got on a ship to escape, but there was a huge storm.	The boat was being rocked by a huge storm.
He said, 'Here I am.'	The sailors threw the man overboard because they thought he had caused the storm.	Jesus walked out on the water towards the boat.
God said, 'Take off your sandals— the ground where you are standing is holy.'	A big fish swallowed the man; he was inside the fish for three nights and three days.	The man was afraid and thought it might be a ghost coming towards them.
God said, 'I have seen how my people are suffering as slaves in Egypt, and I have heard them beg for my help because of the way they are being ill-treated.'	The man realised he should have done what God asked, and he said sorry. The fish spat him out.	The man said, 'Lord, if it is really you, tell me to come to you on the water.'
God told him to go to the king of Egypt and free the Israelite slaves.	God spoke to the man and told him again to go to Nineveh.	Jesus said, 'Come on!'
The man said he was worried about going as he was not a great speaker.	This time the man went to Nineveh.	The man started walking on the water, but became afraid and began to sink.
God said, 'I will be with you.'	The people of Nineveh heeded the man's warning and changed their ways.	Jesus reached out his hand and caught the man, saying, 'Why did you doubt?'

Hearing God's call

Martin Luther King

Martin Luther King lived in America during a time when black people were treated unfairly compared to white people. As a black man, Martin often faced discrimination and harsh treatment. Martin became a church minister in 1948. He said that he did not have a miraculous calling to Christian ministry but felt that God had placed a responsibility on his shoulders, and that he had an inner urge to serve God. In the 1950s, Martin began to fight for equal rights for black people in America. This was a long, hard struggle and was often violent. One night, after yet another threatening phone call, Martin felt like giving up. However, when sitting in his kitchen, he felt he could hear an inner voice of God telling him to keep going, to 'stand up for truth', and that God would be with him. He spent the rest of his life campaigning for the rights of black people.

Jackie Pullinger

Jackie Pullinger had been brought up as a Christian and, from a young age, had felt that she wanted to be a missionary. However, she didn't really know what that meant or what she should do. As she grew up, she was good at music and eventually became a music teacher, but she still felt that she should be doing something else with her life. She prayed often to God, asking what she should be doing, but God never seemed to give her a clear answer.

One night, Jackie had a dream in which she saw herself and her family looking at a map. There was one country that stood out in a different colour: that country was Hong Kong. She still wasn't sure whether God wanted her to go to Hong Kong, so she applied for a teaching job there but was told that there were no jobs. She continued to pray and struggle over what she should do.

One day, at a prayer meeting, she heard someone speaking quietly. She knew that the message was for her: it was, 'Go. Trust me, and I will lead you.' She did trust God but she still did not know where to go or what she should do. A minister she spoke to said that if she had everything worked out, then she wouldn't need to trust God! He told her to get on a boat for the longest journey she could find and pray that she would know where to get off. She did just that and, in 1966, got off the boat at Hong Kong. She stayed there for many years, helping drug addicts and teaching people about Jesus. She made a difference to the lives of thousands of people and has become an inspiration to many.

Reuben

Reuben tells his own story of his calling… 'I left school at 16 with GCSEs and went to study A Levels at the local college. After my first year of A Levels, I received my results and found that I had failed two of my exams. I spoke with my tutor and we came to the conclusion that I should start a new course in Health and Social Care, because I had just started a new job working with people who have learning difficulties. I started the course and loved it, but I still had no sense of direction. Then, in November, I was taken ill and had to go into hospital for a few days. After being in hospital, I thought (and prayed!) about what God wanted me to do, and nursing seemed like a really good idea, so I applied for a new job working as a nursing assistant at the hospital. I loved it! It was the best job I ever had and I learnt loads. I then went forward and applied to university to study Nursing, which is where I am today, studying at the original nursing school started by Florence Nightingale.

'Looking back on it, I can see God preparing me to enter the world of nursing; from my first job through to starting university, everything just seemed right. I see nursing as my ministry among my patients. While on the ward, I carry a holding cross in the pocket of my scrubs to help me to remember to rely on God, even when things are tough.'

Lyn

Lyn was on holiday visiting her friend in September 2005 when she had three dreams. In her first dream she saw a man at the foot of her bed singing a song. The lyrics were, 'Take the shackles off my feet so I can dance.' Later, in a second dream, she was walking down a pavement, passing young people dragging chains and with their heads bent. She clearly heard a voice that said, 'Who will tell them of a God that loves them and a Saviour that cares?' The next night she had a third dream. She was in a car driving into a village. She parked the car, got out and could smell the sea. At the end of a row of shops and houses, she saw a cafe. It had a sign saying, 'Shackles Off', with a picture of broken chains above the door. It was the only building with a light on. Inside were young people in a café, and her friend was serving behind the counter. Lyn felt sure that these dreams were from God.

The next Sunday, she went with her friend to Seascale Methodist Church. As they drove into the village, she recognised it from her dream. On the way home, Lyn's friend pointed to the building at the end of the row of shops and said that she had always felt that God was going to do something there for the young people. This was the café that Lyn had seen in her dream. Eventually, Lyn told her friend about the dreams and, although initially Lyn felt a sense of panic, she knew that God was calling her to do something specific to help the young people of that place. She later moved to Seascale, making the difficult decision to leave her old life behind, and set up the 'Shackles Off' youth project in the place that she had seen in her dream. It is now set up as a café, has many young people who visit the project, and even has a sign above the door saying 'Shackles Off', exactly like the one she saw in her dream.

Would you or wouldn't you?

You are asked by your group leader to help with the weekly litter-pick around the church.	A local preservation society is looking for young people to help plant trees.
A friend has asked you to look after their guinea pig while they are on holiday.	You have been asked to clean your bedroom.
An elderly neighbour needs help mowing their lawn.	Your local playground has a problem with vandalism and the local council is looking for volunteers to help clear it up.
Your church has a weekly coffee morning and is looking for volunteers to help clear the tables.	The young people in your church have been asked to form a worship band or choir.
Your church is looking for volunteers to be on the welcome team rota.	Your church wants to develop a website and is looking for volunteers to help design the site and maintain it.
The local hospital radio station has asked your youth group to help deliver flyers for an annual fundraising event.	The local hospital radio station is looking for new presenters for the children's ward.
Your church's after-school club is looking for volunteers to help younger children with their homework.	Your garden at home needs weeding.
Your neighbour has broken their leg and has asked you if you could walk their dog once a day for six weeks.	Your church has a monthly magazine and is looking for volunteers to contribute regular articles.
The local primary school is looking for keen footballers to come along and teach skills and tactics to their team on Saturday mornings.	You have discovered that there are a number of *Doctor Who* fans in your group at church who want to set up a fan club.
The local drama group is looking for people to be part of their backstage and costumes group.	The local farm or city farm is looking for volunteers to help with the animals.

Gifts and skills

Heart: What do you care about most?	**Abilities**: What talents or gifts do you have?
Heart: What do you love to do?	**Abilities**: What have people said you are good at?
Heart: What are your hopes in life?	**Abilities**: What would you like to be good at?
Heart: What are your ambitions?	**Abilities**: What talent or gift can you teach or share with someone else?
Heart: What would you like to change in the world?	**Abilities**: What talent would you like to learn from someone else?
Heart: What do you like about the world?	**Abilities**: What gifts or talents do you admire in others?
Heart: What really motivates you?	**Abilities**: How do you know what your gifts and talents are?
Personality: What makes you who you are?	**Experience**: What have you learnt?
Personality: What do you think you are like?	**Experience**: What is your favourite experience in life so far?
Personality: What do people say you are like?	**Experience**: What are you an expert in?
Personality: What is your favourite thing about you?	**Experience**: What is experience?
Personality: What did you learn about yourself from the identity sessions?	**Experience**: Can you learn from experience?
Personality: Were you surprised by anything in the identity sessions?	**Experience**: Have you learnt anything from your experiences?

Which task?

Read the tasks below and decide whether or not you would like to have a go at them. Put a smiley face in the column that best matches your answer for each one.

Task	No, thanks	I'll have a go	Yes, but I'll need support	Easy
Find out what is involved in running your church.				
Talk to a group of peers about a subject that interests you.				
Give a presentation to your church on youth culture in your community.				
Chair a meeting.				
Take the minutes at a meeting.				
Facilitate a group discussion.				
Organise a rota.				
Meet and greet people in church.				
Take time to talk to people.				
Organise a litter-pick at your local park.				
Prepare an agenda.				
Organise a community event such as a barbecue, coffee morning or free car wash.				
Research a subject on the internet.				
Be on the reading rota in church.				

Task	No, thanks	I'll have a go	Yes, but I'll need support	Easy
Act as a junior steward.				
Help at a Holy Communion service.				
Help on the sound desk.				
Write prayers of intercessions and deliver them.				
Help with the offertory each week.				
Be part of the welcome team.				
Give the notices at church each week.				
Create a weekly bulletin informing the church about children's and youth ministry.				
Facilitate a youth and children's forum.				
Research what activities go on in the community.				
Plan and run a fundraising event for a local charity.				
Host an all-age event for your church.				
Shadow and help your minister.				
Run a Bible study group.				
Meet with children's or youth workers to help with the strategic planning of children's and youth ministry in your church.				
Act as an advocate for the children in your church or group.				

Task	No, thanks	I'll have a go	Yes, but I'll need support	Easy
Observe and evaluate a session at a youth club or your group.				
Create a website for your church.				
Write an article for a newsletter.				
Plan a service or discussion session on worship for 9- to 14-year-olds.				
Look after the church noticeboard, noticesheet or newsletter.				
Organise a 'bring and share' lunch after church.				
Organise a coffee and chat morning.				
Teach a new song to the congregation.				
Write a press release about an event at your church.				
Design and print posters for a church event or to advertise activities at your church.				
Coordinate elected representatives to liaise with adults on church committees.				
Coach or mentor other young people.				

Questions

Write down the names of everyone who has done, or can do, the following things.

Question	Name(s)
Who volunteered to do something for someone else?	
Who learnt something new about themselves in the sessions?	
Who mentored or taught a new skill to another person?	
Who can give an example of someone in the Bible who responded to God's call?	
Who can think of at least three roles in the church?	
Who can give three examples of things that go on in their community?	
Who can remember the six session titles in order?	
Who can remember one of the Bible passages used in the sessions?	

Growing Young Leaders

A practical guide to mentoring teens

Ruth Hassall

Being a teenager may well be more challenging today than at any time in recent years—and being a Christian teenager presents further challenges. Increasingly, the role of the mentor is being seen as key in helping young people to make right choices and learn to live well, so that they are equipped to find a safe path to maturity.

This book offers practical guidance to those who feel called to mentoring 13–18 year olds in a faith context, with a view to nurturing them towards leadership roles. Linked to CPAS's course *Growing Leaders—Youth Edition*, it also works as a stand-alone resource. It defines mentoring, analyses the necessary skills and attributes of a mentor today, encourages good practice, and above all considers how to help young people identify their gifts and grow as Christian disciples.

ISBN 978 1 84101 637 5   £7.99
Available from your local Christian bookshop or direct from BRF: visit www.brfonline.org.uk

Girls for God: Soul Perspectives

Katie Wood

'Being a teenager is not easy at the best of times. There are so many changes, like moving schools, getting jobs, or even starting university, and there are a lot of stresses too, like exams, arguments and trying to get a boyfriend. Some of this is pretty scary, but a lot of it is really exciting too…

'I have written this book of Bible reflections, thoughts and prayers, because I wanted something similar for myself but couldn't find it. Although I haven't been a Christian for many years, my faith has helped me through a lot and I want to encourage others, especially if they are going through hard times, to stay close to God. I have learned that this is the best way of dealing with anything.

'I am not going to boast about my special qualifications for discussing these kinds of issues because I don't have any—apart from being a teenager myself. What I do have, though, is experience. I wrote this book while studying at sixth form, worrying about universities and stressing about my friends. I hope that this book gives you some help and inspiration to keep you going as a Christian—or to show you the difference that knowing God can make, if you are wondering if it is worth getting acquainted!'

ISBN 0 85746 070 7   £6.99
Available from your local Christian bookshop or direct from BRF: visit www.brfonline.org.uk

Side by Side with God in Everyday Life

Helping children to grow with God through all times

Yvonne Morris

Side by Side with God in Everyday Life invites churches and families alike to use a simple retelling of stories from the Bible as the basis for helping children aged 6–10 to think more deeply about a wide range of everyday topics.

In total there are 28 easy-to-use story-based sessions, each one featuring one of the times and seasons outlined in Ecclesiastes 3:1–8, such as birth, death, planting, uprooting, laughing, mourning, dancing, giving, listening, love, hate, war and peace.

Each session picks out two related Bible stories, one to set the scene and the other to go deeper into the theme. The idea is that these simple retellings can be used to promote open questions, reflection, discussion, further exploration and prayer, and readily act as prompts towards a deeper understanding of what it means to walk side by side with God in everything we do.

ISBN 978 1 84101 855 3   £7.99
Available from your local Christian bookshop or direct from BRF: visit www.brfonline.org.uk

Enjoyed
this book?

Write a review—we'd love to hear what you think. Email: reviews@brf.org.uk

Keep up to date—receive details of our new books as they happen.
Sign up for email news and select your interest groups at:
www.brfonline.org.uk/findoutmore/

Follow us on Twitter @brfonline

By post—to receive new title information by post (UK only), complete the form below and post to: BRF Mailing Lists, 15 The Chambers, Vineyard, Abingdon, Oxfordshire, OX14 3FE

Your Details

Name _____

Address_____

_____

Town/City _____   Post Code _____

Email _____

Your Interest Groups (*Please tick as appropriate)

☐ Advent/Lent

☐ Bible Reading & Study

☐ Children's Books

☐ Discipleship

☐ Leadership

☐ Messy Church

☐ Pastoral

☐ Prayer & Spirituality

☐ Resources for Children's Church

☐ Resources for Schools

Support your local bookshop
Ask about their new title information schemes.